Motor Activity and
The Education of Retardates

Motor Activity and The

Education of Retardates

BRYANT J. CRATTY, Ed.D.

Professor and Director, Perceptual-Motor Learning Laboratory, Department of Physical Education, University of California, Los Angeles

Lea & Febiger   Philadelphia, 1969

Health Education,
Physical Education, and
Recreation Series

RUTH ABERNATHY, Ph.D., EDITORIAL ADVISER
Chairman, Department for Women, School of Physical and Health Education, University of Washington, Seattle, Washington, 98105.

to Madeleine

Preface

Traditionally, the inclusion of physical activities in educational programs for normal children has been justified in so far as exercise apparently produces vigor, better postural adjustment, and supplies an enjoyable break from classroom drudgeries. It is not surprising, therefore, that when physical education programs were devised for retarded children that activities reflecting similar rationale were formulated.

I believe, however, that properly planned programs of motor activity can make more important contributions to the total development of a retarded child than simply making his muscles larger, correcting a low shoulder, or supplying a measure of fun. I have attempted in this book to demonstrate just how movement may aid a retarded child to function better with his family, in the classroom, and with his neighborhood friends.

While the pages of this text, at times, contain comments critical of some of the contemporary theoretical statements regarding intellectual-motor relationships, it is believed that some of the writers mentioned have made important contributions to special education by focusing the attention of teachers and administrators upon the obvious behavior children evidence in their movements. I hope, however, that the text will forestall both an evangelical over-reaction to the purported curative powers of motor activity sometimes seen in the unsophisticated, as well as the rejection of movement programs in schools which have also been observed with increasing frequency on the part of some special educators. The prevention of an over-acceptance, or a "backlash" rejection, has been attempted by delineating, as precisely as currently available research evidence permits, just how motor activities may be helpful in school programs for children with learning difficulties; as well as by providing cautions, similarly based upon "hard" data, which suggest that movement is only one component of the child's personality and not the basis from which all social, intellectual, emotional, and perceptual attributes stem. I have tried to sort facts and intelligent speculation from fallacies by shifting statements about movement behavior through a fine sieve of data provided by researchers in the behavioral sciences. At times, when data were not available, it was possible to obtain material using the research staff in my own laboratory. Thus, the text contains findings of studies specifically carried on to provide material for this book. Examples of this are information dealing with the self-concept, games-choice, pre-post test results of a program of motor training, and norms for figure drawing.

It was desired that readers having a diversity of backgrounds gain helpful information from the contents of this text. The research scholar may be particularly interested in the review of the literature containing a critical discussion of current theories and practices, suggestions for needed research as well as a reasonably comprehensive bibliography. The curriculum specialist, school psychologist, and supervisors of special education and physical education may be aided in the information of valid testing and screening instruments by referring to the norms within Chapters 4 and 6, as well as the test contained in the Appendix.

Parents and classroom teachers may wish to ''skim'' some of the more technical portions of the book, but should derive some benefit from reviewing the techniques and games contained in Chapters 6 to 9. It is hoped, however, that practitioners will not totally ignore the theoretical underpinnings of the practices they adopt, for to do so will limit their own creative energies and flexibility, as well as creating the individual, too often seen working with children, who ''does'' but does not know why!

Many individuals aided in the compilation of materials contained in this book. Sister Margaret Mary Martin, chairman of the Physical Education Department at Alverno College contributed her excellent editorial skills when reviewing the manuscript. I have been able to take advantage of her administrative abilities as well as her mature insights during the past year she has spent with me supervising the clinic program at University of California at Los Angeles.

The material in the text is based upon data collected from over 2,000 children during the past three years taking part in a dozen research studies. To them, also, gratitude is extended.

Dr. Madeline Hunter, principal of University of California at Los Angeles's University Elementary School, and her staff cooperated with me by permitting her students to be tested. The norms for figure drawing and gross-motor tests are based upon their scores. I would like to thank Dr. Hunter and her staff for their hospitality during the past two years.

Dr. Ernest P. Willenberg, Director of Special Education for the Los Angeles City Schools, and his staff have extended their wholehearted support during the past four years, and have permitted me to work with children in the schools, refining the techniques and games contained in the text. Special thanks are also extended to Miss Shirley Wolk, Mrs. Della Blakeway, Dr. William Hirsch, Mrs. Helen Roberts, Mrs. Rhoda Freeman, Mr. Maurice Moriarity, Miss Rosalie Calone, Mr. Fred Lull, and Mrs. Schweinfest, principals of schools for the physically and mentally handicapped within the Los Angeles City Schools who have extended me their hospitality during the past several years. Mrs. Diane Leichman and Dr. Dorothy Carr, supervisors of special education for Los Angeles City were also cooperative, and their interest has been reflected in the addition of twelve new physical education teachers to their staff during the past year.

Mr. Barry Preiss, Miss Cherie Ritchie, Miss Trish Spradlin and Miss Janet Zeller collected data resulting in norms for drawing behavior, and gross-motor ability, contained in Chapters 4 and 6. Mr. Martin Wilner supervised the research in which the games-choice test was normed, through the cooperation of principal Jack Macey and his staff of teachers at the Montebellow School District in Los Angeles County.

Mr. Thomas Durkin, Mr. John Kaufman, and Mr. Jeffrey Drucker tested children within our Clinic program at University of California at Los Angeles upon which much of the information contained in the text was based. Mrs. Jane Durkin and Mr. Drucker aided in the reduction of data and in the preparation of the Appendix and references. Mrs. Kathleen Fujimoto contributed her excellent typing and editorial skills in the production of the final manuscript.

It is believed that the manuscript is enhanced immeasureably by the technically and artistically well-executed drawings. My thanks for this contribution are extended to the illustrator, Miss Lynn Vander Velde.

Final thanks are also extended to the numerous retarded children from whom I learned so much during the past years in the numerous games we enjoyed playing together.

BRYANT J. CRATTY

Los Angeles, California

Contents

1

Introduction

The affluent American society of the late 1960's has taken critical looks at some of its more unfortunate members. Some of this interest has been prompted by threat as well as by necessity. Racial problems are being examined and programs instituted which will aid in their solution. Children of the poor are introduced to head start programs; the American Indian and the Mexican-American finally have become the focus of federal and local programs.

It is not surprising that concern about the education of retardates and the amelioration of retardation has increased. While biochemists attempt to probe the causes of mental deficiency at the cellular level, behavioral scientists have renewed their attack on the learning and cognitive problems of the less able child and adult.

Children scattered along the intellectual continuum are being provided services in schools. The educationally handicapped child, with an I.Q. within the normal range but lacking the emotional and/or perceptual capacities to learn, is being placed in segregated programs. The severely retarded child is being accepted into the regular schools system to receive special instruction, instead of being relegated to custodial care in mental hospitals. In several areas, the older retardate has been removed from mental hospitals and has been exposed to recreational and cultural programs. In some cases, the results have been astonishingly good.

Paralleling these attempts to better educate more of the group categorized as uneducables are efforts to discover better methodologies for helping them learn. The importance of optimum arousal, orientation to the task, and the diminution of extraneous and interfering motor activity has become the concern of some. Others have employed reinforcement schedules formerly only found in the research laboratory. Reinforcers such as interest in the task, social approval, and bits of candy have been used in many programs with success.

Some schools are organizing "block" programs for the retarded, similar to those found on the secondary level for the normal child. One teacher may be placed in charge of speech, a second engages in vocational training, while a third may be a specialist in the teaching of social skills.

A search is being conducted to discover the way in which various kinds of sensory cues can be employed to offer more palatable and vivid experiences to the child with learning difficulties. To an increased degree, structured and/or unstructured programs of motor activity are being proposed to help the retarded child to learn.

The retardate seldom reflects upon past experiences or attends to the future; he is more concerned with his immediate situation. Momentarily he is motivated by his emotions rather than by reflecting on his long range goals. Movement activities provide this immediate and obvious experience as well as providing an overt and accessible way of evaluating the quality of some of a retardate's thought processes.

Activities involving movement of the limbs and of the total body seem to synthesize a number of types of sensory information. As a child walks a line, he receives sensory feedback from his muscular efforts; as he watches his feet and/or the line, the visual and motor input are integrated. If simultaneously with his visual and motor activity, he must respond to a verbal command ("walk backward on the line"), the structured activity forces him to integrate a third cue into his activity.

Games and less structured motor activities may help a child with learning difficulties adjust his level of excitation to optimums necessary for the performance of less physical tasks. Motor activities designed to slow down and relax the hyperactive child may induce him to exercise self-control when it is needed in the classroom (for example, asking a child to walk a line as slowly as possible).

In contrast to activities designed to reduce tension, others are used to arouse him. The vivid flag-waving and rhythmics suggested by some may motivate and excite the child who is virtually out of contact with reality so that he becomes aware of what is occurring around him. The perpetually "sleepy" child may thus be "awakened" through the excitement of some motor activity or by tactual stimulation.

Special educators are becoming increasingly interested in motor activities for children with learning problems, because they are aware of the retardate's favorable response to movement activities. Movement tasks may provide a means through which a retardate may "act out" his thought processes; and the quality of this "acting out" may be easily assessed by the observing teacher.

Accompanying this interest, and frequently this happens with new ideas in education, there has been a tendency to over-react to the importance of movement in programs for retardates. Motor learning is represented by some theorists as the basis of *all* learning; while others suggest that a number of perceptual attributes may be improved by encouraging a child to move.

Such comprehensive claims for motor activities, while welcomed by some, eventually may result in a black-lash in special education programs. This type of statement is often overly simplistic. Motor activities may be *one* method for aiding *some* children to express choice behavior and to improve other components of cognitive behavior, but only if the participants are encouraged to *think* about their movements. Motor activities may help some children remediate certain visual-perceptual distortions, but they are not a cure for all perceptual deficits in all children.

It is important also to consider the individual differences among retardates in the way they perceive, move, and learn. Motor activities, for example, may be more helpful to the retarded child from the family high on the economic scale, who has been over-protected and has been denied movement experiences. On the other hand, the child from the less privileged communities may lack verbal-linguistic stimulation, but he may function in a superior way in motor tasks, because his environment has forced him to find his own forms of play.

The "label" retardate is applied to children whose learning difficulties may stem from a variety of causes. Because some children are unable to control their levels of activation, they do not focus their attention on anything long enough to acquire important percepts and concepts. Another group of children process information more slowly than the so-called average child, so they are classified as retardates. A third group may have ocular malfunctions which interfere with the gathering of information. Retardation in other children may be caused by subtle and little understood malfunctions in the biochemical makeup of their brain tissue; while others may possess deep seated anatomical abnormalities which result in their inability to learn and to retain.

Such a variety of causes for learning problems in children must be met with teaching strategies that are differentiated and appropriate to the cause. The application of "blanket" methodologies intended to improve perceptual-motor malfunctions is not always appropriate.

Significant evidence is available to demonstrate that some programs in motor education have improved a child's self-concept to the extent that he has gained confidence in his ability to succeed in the classroom. The confidence he gained in motor tasks seems to have affected his performance in intellectual tasks.

But the research studies, relating to improvement in his I.Q. tests after participating in motor education programs, usually fail to specify the reasons for these changes. Thus, the intervening variables between the program of motor education and the change in the intellectual competencies of the subjects need to be identified.

Scholarly and objective researchers have an obligation to the readers of their studies to delineate the actual reasons producing the change in the intellectual ability of the population studied.

Important to a consideration of what programs effect what components of the personalities of both normal and retarded youngsters is an examination of the nature of the aptitudinal structure of both types of children. Correlative studies demonstrate that a retarded child evidences a trait structure which is less fragmented and differentiated than is that of a normal child of like age.

The I.Q. scores of trainable retardates when compared to their motor ability scores usually elicit higher correlations than when the same scores obtained from educable retardates and from normal children are contrasted. The reasons for these higher correlations on the part of children with lower intellectual endowments are probably at least two-fold. These children have not been able to profit from the variety of experiences to which they have been exposed as are normal children. Their aptitude pattern is relatively even which probably reflects the influence more of inherent characteristics than of environmental variables. At the same time, the

I.Q. of children with poor intellectual-verbal competencies are generally assessed primarily by measuring their perceptual-motor attributes, as indeed these measures are the only ones obtainable from such children.

Conversely, when studying a population of normal children, and gradually increasing the complexity of the motor tasks compared to measures of intelligence, higher relationships will be obtained. It is important to remember, however, that such relationships described in these two paragraphs do not infer causality, but only afford basic information pertaining to the manner in which ability attributes in the human personality are arranged and become differentiated as maturation takes place or as the subjects surveyed become intellectually more capable.

The findings of correlative studies comparing intellectual, perceptual-motor and/or fitness scores of retardates may tell very little about the possibility of transfer occurring between the two types of attributes evaluated. Transfer between motor task performance and some percept or concept will occur generally if two conditions can be met: (*a*) bridges of understanding must be built between the motor task and the concept; (*b*) a sufficient number of motor tasks intended to inculcate a given concept must be engaged in.

An example of the application of *a* above may be drawn from the concept that space (and thus letters and numbers) may have a left-right orientation. It has been found that teaching children many left-right things, movements, and such will not necessarily lessen letter and number reversals, unless the concepts involving the correct printing of the number and letter are taught for operationally. The teacher must alert Johnny how "the 'D' faces toward your right hand," rather than simply assuming that if Johnny salutes the flag with his correct hand each morning, the dimensions of his space field will magically organize itself into a left and a right.

At the same time, if Johnny is taught only one left-right game he will usually acquire the ability to play only that game, but his knowledge of the left and right of things will stop at that point. He will probably fail to transfer the concept that his left and right is in any way related to the left and right in space, and that one must align certain things within these exact spatial dimensions. A study carried out two years ago revealed many retarded children who, when asked to do so, could accurately slide their left and right hands above their heads when lying on a mat, but were unable to make any other left-right judgments better than would be expected by chance.

The separation of perceptual, cognitive, and motor abilities and attitudinal tendencies is not a simple matter. Any attempt to influence one component of the human personality by tasks lying within another attribute cluster is not easily accomplished. A retarded child, for example, may not place letters and words in their correct left-right dimensions, simply because he does not believe that it makes any difference! A normal four- or five-year-old child will often evidence this same lack of concern for the spatial arrangement of numbers and letters.

The evaluation of the retarded child's motor abilities may be corrupted by his inability to give *himself* effective directions and/or to process the directions given him by an examiner. For example, when asking a retarded child to see how long he can remain standing on one foot, it is not unusual to find that he will stand with his feet wide apart, inscribing the letter "A" with his lower limbs. Starting from this broad base, he will attempt to raise one foot from the ground, and failing to do so, he will give up, and will thus receive a low balance score from the tester.

Many times, however, if this same child is instructed *how* to stand on one foot (*i.e.,* place the correct hip over the foot remaining on the ground, with the accompanying weight shift), frequently he can posture quite well in the position requested. Thus separation, in this case, of the child's basic balancing ability from his intellect, as reflected in the work method he selected when doing the balance task, is a difficult undertaking.

With these cautions in mind, I believe there are several ways in which motor activities, if properly applied, may contribute to the total education of retarded children.

1. Movement tasks, designed to arouse or calm, may enable a child to achieve a level of arousal appropriate to classroom tasks with which he is confronted.

2. Movement experiences help retarded children to exercise more self-control, and to focus their attention for longer periods of time on tasks at hand.

3. Lead-up activities involving hand-eye coordination tasks will enable the retardate to effectively transcribe his thoughts to paper and to draw with more facility.

4. To a large extent vocational opportunities for retarded children and young adults involve competency in motor task performance. Improvement in motor abilities appropriate to proficiencies needed in industry should increase chances of employment.

5. A retarded child may be helped to better structure space by engaging in movement tasks in which spatial concepts are inculcated.

6. Rhythmic activities may aid a retarded child to organize time, to speak, to read, and to write more efficiently.

7. Improvement of the generally low fitness levels of retardates may be achieved in well-motivated programs of physical activity.

8. Certain basic components of intellectual processes involving choice-making, categorizing, and seriation may be "acted-out" in movement tasks.

9. Mathematics and spelling skills may be improved by engaging in movement activities.

10. The general self-concept of retardates may be improved by successful experiences in physical education activities which in turn may positively influence their level of aspiration and performance on other types of tasks to which they are exposed.

11. The motivating nature of motor activities may be utilized to improve the linguistic and verbal skills of children with learning difficulties.

Perceptual-motor activities, however, should not constitute the totality of the educational program for the retardate. Speech training, social skills, cognitive exercises, and specific vocational education should be emphasized when appropriate.

SUMMARY

To an increased degree, movement experiences are being utilized in the educational programs for retardates. While at times there is an over-reaction to the curative powers of movement, with careful planning and correct application, motor task performance may have a positive effect upon some of the perceptual, intellectual, and emotional attributes of some children with learning difficulties.

Motor activities, if administered appropriately, may aid a hyperactive child to place himself under better control and conversely may tend to activate the phlegmatic child. Motor proficiency, when improved, may exert a concomitant improvement in a retardate's chances for vocational success. Improvement in movement accuracy enables the child to transcribe with more efficiency his thoughts to paper, while a heightened ability to participate in games with success will often improve the general self-concept of the child with learning problems.

Movement tasks, when properly directed and motivated, may aid in certain components of cognitive behavior. Seriation, categorization, response generalization and the like may be "acted-out" in various movement tasks. Practice of this nature enables the observing teacher to evaluate the quality of a child's thought processes and to increase the complexity of these activities. Movement will not magically change the intellect, unless the movements engaged in are arranged in proper order and are thought about. Movement will not alter the totality termed, perception. But motor tasks, if properly applied, may change some perceptual attributes.

REFERENCES

1. Brown, Roscoe C.: "The Effect of a Perceptual-Motor Education Program on Perceptual-Motor Skills and Reading Readiness," Presented at Research Section, AAHPER, St. Louis, Missouri, April 1, 1968.
2. Cratty, Bryant J.: *The Perceptual-Motor Attributes of Mentally Retarded Children and Youth,* (Monograph), Mental Retardation Services Board, Los Angeles County, 1966.
3. Duffy, Elizabeth: *Activation and Behavior,* New York: John Wiley & Sons, Inc., 1962.
4. Elkin, Edwin H. and Friedman, Erwin: *Development of Basic Motor Abilities Tests for Retardates: A Feasibility Study,* (Monograph), Jointly Funded by the American Institutes for Research and the Jewish Foundation for Retarded Children, Inc., 1967.
5. Gearheart, Bill R.: "A Study of a Physical Education Program Designed to Promote Motor Skills of Educable Mentally Retarded Children Enrolled in Special Education Classes in Cedar Rapids, Iowa," Research Study No. 1, Dissertation Abstracts *25*(1), 271–272.
6. Ghent, L. and Bernstein, L.: "Effect of Orientation On Recognition of Geometric Forms by Retarded Children," *Child Devel.; 35,* 1127–1136, 1964.
7. Gibson, E. J., and Gibson, J. J., Pick, A. I., and Oseer, H. A.: "A Developmental Study of the Discrimination of Letter-Like Forms," *J. Comp. Physiol. Psych.; 55,* 897–906, 1962.
8. Hill, S. D., McCullum, A. H., and Sceau, A.: "Relation of Training in Motor Activity to Development of Left-Right Directionality in Mentally Retarded Children: Exploratory Study," *Percept. & Mot. Skills; 24,* 363–366, 1967.
9. Humphrey, James H.: "Comparison of the Use of Active Games and Language Workbook Exercises as Learning Media in the Development of Language Understandings With Third Grade Children," *Percept. & Mot. Skills; 21,* 23–26, 1965.

10. Jacobson, Edmund: Anxiety and Tension Control—*A Physiological Approach,* Philadelphia, J. B. Lippincott Co., 1964.

11. Johnson, G. Orville: "A Study of the Social Position of Mentally Handicapped Children in the Regular Grades," *Am. J. Ment. Defic.; 55,* 60–89, 1950.

12. Kagan, Jerome: "Body Build and Conceptual Impulsivity In Children," *J. Person.; 34,* 118–128, 1966.

13. Leighton, J. M., Cupp, A., Prince, D. Philabaum, G., MclArren: "The Effect of a Physical Fitness Development Program on Self-Concept, Mental Age, and Job Proficiency In the Mentally Retarded," *J. of Physio. and Ment. Rehab.; 20,* 4–11, 1966.

14. Mosston, Muska: *Teaching Physical Education—From Command to Discovery,* Columbus, Ohio, Charles E. Merrill Books, Inc., 1966.

15. Neale, Marie D.: "Perceptual Development of Severely Retarded Children Through Motor Experience," *J. Ment. Subnormality,* (Monograph), April, 1966.

16. ———: "The Effects of a Broad Art and Movement Program Upon a Group of 'Trainable' Retarded Children," International Copenhagen Congress on the Scientific Study of Mental Retardation, Denmark, 7–14, August, 1964.

17. Oliver, J. N.: "The Effect of Physical Conditioning Exercises and Activities on the Mental Characteristics of Educationally Sub-Normal Boys," *Br. J. Ed. Psychol.; 28,* 155–165, June, 1958.

18. Robbins, Melvyn P.: "The Delacato Interpretation of Neurological Organization," *Read. Res. Quart.; I,* 57–78, Spring, 1966.

19. Semmel, M. I.: "Arousal Theory and Vigilance Behavior of Educable Mentally Retarded and Average Children," *Am. J. Ment. Defic.; 70,* 38–47, 1965.

20. Solomon, A., and R. Prangle: "Demonstrations of Physical Fitness Improvement in the EMR," *Except. Child.; 33,* 177–181, November, 1967.

21. Weatherford, R. S., and Harrocks, John: "Peer Acceptance and Over and Under Achievement in School," *J. Psychol.; 66,* 215–220, 1964.

22. Zeaman, D. and House, Betty J.: "The Role of Attention in Retardate Discrimination Learning," in *Handbook of Mental Deficiency,* N. R. Ellis (Ed.), New York, McGraw-Hill Book Co., 159–553, 1963.

2

Research, Motor Activity, and the Retardate

It is often difficult for school administrators and for teachers to separate valid from spurious inferences surrounding any new trend in education. Interpretation of literature purporting to explain the manner in which movement experiences may be integrated into the educational programs of children with learning difficulties is particularly difficult. Many educators have been bombarded with literature containing positive statements based upon no objective evidence. Frequently it is difficult for teachers to obtain copies of sound research investigations emerging from the laboratories of thoughtful behavioral scientists which shed light upon movement-mental relationships.

Two basic inaccuracies prevail within the pronouncements surrounding the place of movement in education. Frequently heard are statements, such as, more research is needed to . . . , followed by a sentence which reveals that the speaker is unaware of the vast number of studies which *do* exist dealing with the problem in question.* The second fallacy is exemplified by an often simplistic pronouncement which purports to quickly and easily explain a complex process (*i.e.,* thinking, reading, and perception).

Within the investigations which have been carried out often lie several dangers. The Placebo effect may be present, the positive suggestion inserted by an innovator which tends to enhance the effects of some technique when researched by the creator or by a devoted disciple. The Hawthorn effect, the built-in advantage that the new and interesting experimental procedures have over the familiar and often boring procedures usually applied to the controls may exert a confounding influence upon the findings. A third problem is the tendency to make broad generalizations from results obtained from small and often ill-defined groups of sub-

---

*Two of my recent texts contain bibliographies which together list almost 1500 references[19], while a text by Howard and Templeton[41] contains an additional 1600 research articles and books dealing with perception, motion, and thought.

jects. Additionally, a researcher is often tempted to utilize statistical methods which will maximize the possibility of finding statistically significant differences.[43]

It is unnecessary for an educator to find a research article which supports *every* facet of his educational program. Some things which are done may just make "good sense." At the same time, the scientific method of problem solving, whether applied in action situations (the playground and classroom), or within the research laboratory, is a helpful way to evaluate new practices and to mold those presently in use into better teaching tools. I encourage readers to adopt a critical attitude toward some of the suggestions developed in this book. It is thus hoped that the review of the literature which follows will support a scholarly appraisal of the material presented in the chapters which follow.

Several primary concepts should be kept in mind when dealing with practices purported to improve retardate learning. (a) The causes for retardation are many and varied; thus the methods for utilizing whatever learning capacities an individual child possesses should be varied and applied in a flexible manner. (b) An individual retardate may adopt various strategies to deal with his environment or to reject it. Thus research in which group scores may be compared after some kind of group learning experience may not provide information which is helpful when dealing with a single child with learning difficulties. (c) While many retardates may be similar to a normal child of a younger age, there are basic differences between the way their attributes cluster. (d) There are other causes for learning difficulties which are independent of the sensory and/or motor deficits of a retarded child. It is apparent, therefore that some kind of motor training will not aid the general learning of all retarded children.

When comparing the scores collected from a variety of measures obtained from trainable retardates, relatively high inter-correlations are frequently obtained. Educables subjected to the same analysis usually evidence scores which are not as highly related to one another. By the time a normal child reaches the age of eight or nine, it is extremely difficult to predict his score on one test of motor ability from those obtained from a second test of motor ability.[14,21]

There are several probable causes for this increased fragmentation of attributes as normal children get older and/or the population surveyed is intellectually more capable; and several implications for the education of retardates arise from this type of finding. The severely retarded child, unable to profit very much from experience, continues to evidence stable and low ability on any task with which he is confronted. His scores in a variety of measures are probably more of a reflection of inherent factors than of environmental variables. A second reason for moderate to high correlations between mental and motor tests among retarded children is the primary way in which the so-called mental attributes of retarded children are evaluated is through their performance in perceptual-motor tasks.

The review of the literature will examine several types of research. Initially, rather broad topics will be surveyed, including movement-intellect and perceptual-motor relationships. The review will conclude with analyses of sub-topics, including the influence of attention and arousal upon retardate learning, and an analysis of visual-motor training. The chapter concludes with a summary of the research and with suggestions for further study which should prove illuminating.

MOVEMENT AND THE INTELLECT

Studies in which motor activity has been linked to cognitive functions are of three primary types. (*a*) Correlative studies, (*b*) experimental studies investigating causal relationships, and (*c*) research in the manner in which infants acquire intellectual attributes, and perceptual abilities.

Correlative Studies. In the main studies comparing motor and mental attributes, carried out over the years, point to low, but at times significant, correlations between the two attributes.[3,7] Occasionally, however, a scholar has claimed that these low correlations confirm the fact that there is a motor base to the intellect; and/or that participation in physical activity will improve academic performance and I.Q.[50] When reviewing such studies, it must be kept in mind that a correlation does not necessarily infer that one attribute, if improved, will change the other. If a moderate correlation is obtained between a motor task and an I.Q. score, it usually infers that some degree of thought is necessary when performing the movement.

For example, studies of retardates have been carried out in which a score in a simple motor act (jump and reach) has been contrasted to I.Q., with no significant relationship obtained. However, when a score of a four-count task (squat . . . thrust to a push-up position, return to a squat and rise) was compared to an I.Q. test, a moderate relationship emerged.[26] It is obvious that the second motor act involved the same ability to remember a series of directions as do many items of an intelligence test.

Ismail and Gruber,[50] in a recent monograph, obtained small correlations between I.Q. measures and motor tasks in which about five items of information had to be remembered by the performing child (*i.e.,* "Hop twice on your left foot, then hop twice on your right without hesitation."). It was only when low achieving children were utilized as subjects that even these slight correlations were uncovered (.3 and .4 indicating a common variance of only from 9 to 16 per cent).

Little justification for the statement that motor learning is the basis of all learning or that movement is the basis of the intellect can be gained from correlative studies of this nature, if one accepts the rationale upon which the intellectual measures and motor performance measures are based.

When claims are made that a relationship exists between motor performance and intelligence, a careful delineation must be made of the exact complexity of the motor tasks used in the comparison. If a population of normal children is used, and one begins contrasting motor tasks of increasing complexity with their intelligence scores, increasingly higher correlations result. These findings suggest that movement, *per se*, is not the base from which *all* human attributes emerge. Rather the findings simply confirm the fact that the performance of most motor tasks is dependent to some degree upon thought. Thus, one might conclude that to improve a child's thought processes through movement, one must encourage and stimulate the child to think about his movements.

Muska Mosston supports these conclusions in his theory of a spectrum of teaching styles.[67] Taking a position similar to that advanced by several scholars interested in cognitive processes Mosston holds that true learning takes place only if the child has some control over decisions permeating the learning environment.

He contends that a stimulus-response type of learning is not appropriate for the optimum development of the human intellect.

Mosston suggests that a gradual transfer of decision making from the instructor to the learner should be paced according to the child's ability to assume the responsibility for making decisions when it is felt that the child is capable. According to him, teachers should proceed from situations in which the teacher issues commands governing the behavior of the learner to situations in which the learner is permitted to make decisions about modifying the task and the evaluation. Later, providing the teacher thinks the child is capable of doing it, he is allowed to make those decisions which the teacher usually reserves for himself, *i.e.,* the nature of the activity to meet certain goals.

Unfortunately, this methodology, while being used in regular classroom learning, has not received extensive attention by experimentalists interested in retarded children. Studies carried out on normal children, in which behaviors elicited by the traditional command-teaching was compared to those elicited by this problem-solving approach, indicated that students subjected to the latter methodology evidenced more flexible response patterns which accommodated to the changing complexities of the game strategy which developed. Students taught skill specifics learned these skills more exactly and quickly than the others, but they lacked this flexibility of response.[94]

It is believed that the methodology espoused by Mosston has important implications for the education of retardates. What could be more encouraging to educators than to observe a retardate quietly thinking about a "movement problem" presented to him by his teacher. Activities dealing with this type of learning experience are described in Chapter 11.

Investigations of Causality. A second type of evidence, important to consider in this context, has arisen from studies made to determine the causative effects of a physical activity program on measures of intelligence. Some of these studies examined the effects of the structured movement programs espoused by Doman-Delacato.[23] Other studies have combined simple locomotor tasks with visual training and the use of reflex-like movements.[57,64] Additional research has explored the influence of traditional physical education programs on scores of academic achievement and intelligence.[69,17,60,88]

At times their methodologies and conclusions may be questioned. One, for example excluded an undisclosed number of subjects from the study if their teacher thought the I.Q. scores obtained were invalid.[50] Another concluded that one of the movement theories was tenable, even though more improvement was elicited in a wide variety of perceptual-motor tasks on the part of his *control* group.[57] Another experimenter utilized only eight subjects in his experimental group.[17]

In general the findings of these investigations point to the need for delineating more precisely the nature of the population to whom motor activities are applied and for the better control of the variables which might have influenced change. Identification of intervening variables such as improved self-concept or increased physical stamina are necessary because of their possible affects upon learning capabilities of a child.

Scholars, concerned with the emerging concept of individual differences in learning, should be heeded by researchers interested in describing the possible influence of motor activity upon intellectual potential and academic achievement.[34] An example in point is the study of James Oliver who found that he could improve by 25 per cent the I.Q.'s of educable retardates by subjecting them to an extra three hours a day of physical activity in which they learned recreational skills and participated in fitness activities. Dr. Oliver speculated that the improvement elicited stemmed from a heightened motivational state and an improved self-concept.[69]

Corder similarly found improvement in I.Q. was elicited by a program of physical education. In Corder's study, one group was inserted which interacted socially with the experimental "physical education" group to control for the well-known "Hawthorn Effect" (the influence of personal attention and experimenter rapport upon the measures of behavioral change obtained).[17] In a more definitive investigation completed by Solomon and Prangle, however, it was found that improvement in a retardate population subjected to a special physical education program was obtained only in motor ability, with I.Q. and other measures of school achievement remaining unaffected.[88]

These conflicting findings probably arise from a failure to delineate the personality trait structures, learning strategies, and similar factors within the groups studied. Oliver's subjects may have suffered from a lack of self-confidence when performing motor activities; when their skill improved, they blossomed. Whereas, Solomon and Prangle may have used self-confident children who felt comfortable in motor activities before they began experimenting with them.

It is sometimes forgotten that many things happen to experimental subjects before the researcher enters their lives to insert, usually for a brief period of time, something which it is hoped will change them in some way. It is this assumption which influences the type of findings usually obtained in studies of transfer of training when normal subjects are utilized; the transfer to the second activity has usually happened in the subjects' lives long before they participated in the experiment for a few minutes a day.

A review of the literature makes it apparent that retarded children are rejected by their more capable peers, not only because of the perceived intellectual differences, but because their frustrations may lead toward unacceptable aggressive social behaviors.[52] Similarly, the retardate who perceives himself unable to perform motor tasks as well as his normal companions appears to give up trying to improve by late childhood. Because of this withdrawal, frequently he will regress in his ability to perform a variety of perceptual-motor skills as he reaches adolescence.[21, 14]

The findings of the study by Zeaman and Orlando produced similar results. A "failure-set" was instilled in retarded children by confronting them with unsolvable tasks. Following this failure experience, the children were unable or unwilling to solve simpler problems which previously they had accomplished easily.[99]

Taken together, these findings make it apparent that increased proficiency in skill may not only provide a socially acceptable way in which a retardate may interact with his own kind and with normal youngsters. If continued success is realized, it may encourage him to continue his participation, resulting in continued enhancement of his perceptual-motor development as he grows from childhood into young adulthood.

The findings of studies in which more structured movement programs have been inserted are not usually supportive of their worth in the educational program. Kershner[57] concluded that a perceptual-motor theory was supported when, after a program of crawling, his experimental subjects improved in crawling and in a picture identification test of I.Q., despite the fact that his control group improved more in a battery of perceptual-motor tasks (termed the Kershner revision of the Oseretsky), than did his experimental subjects! Other studies purporting to support the Doman-Delacato program of movement education are similarly questionable in content and methodology. One reviewer has suggested they are distinguished only by "their faults."[38]

Robbins, in investigating the influence of the Doman-Delacato program upon the subjects' ability to distinguish left from right, to read, and to form other perceptual judgments, found that the program exerted no significant influence upon the attributes tested.[77] Laterality was not improved significantly in a program which stressed left-right and unilateral motor activity, according to Robbins' findings. His investigation is one of the few in which proper controls were utilized to study this program of motor training.

The reluctance of Doman and Delacato to subject their methods to experimental verification has made some members of the medical profession skeptical of their worth.[96] The extraordinary physical demands made upon the child and his family are similarly questioned by leading pediatricians, neurologists, and psychiatrists.[96]

It is possible that some children may benefit from the Doman-Delacato method of increasing their mobility. However, to subject all children with learning problems to such a strenuous program of extensive and prolonged physical therapy is open to question. An effort should be made to learn just what kind of child is being dealt with, and in what ways can the child improve under the conditions of the program, if indeed any improvement may be elicited on the part of any child under the conditions described in the literature outlining the methodology.[23,24]

The influence of the program espoused by Kephart[56] has also been scrutinized with varying degrees of sophistication. In a recent definitive study by Brown[9] it was found that while certain measures of perception were improved, after engaging in the tasks Kephart suggests, no significant improvement in reading scores was forthcoming.* Other researchers studying the effects of training procedures espoused by Kephart have published findings which are not much more promising. Rutherford studied the effect of Kephart activities on the Metropolitan Readiness Test scores of kindergarten children finding a significant gain for the boys but not for the girls. LaPray and Ross, using first graders who were low in both reading and visual perception found that one group after being trained in simple

---

*Scholars should probably place more faith in findings produced by experimenters without an obvious emotional commitment to the various programs and by those not in close physical proximity to the various facilities in which these programs take place, as exemplified by the investigations by Robbins[76] and Brown.[9] If advocates of the various programs engage in research purporting to establish their worth, it is like the brother of a drug manufacturer researching a drug without the traditional double-blind precautions traditional in such research.

reading materials improved in reading, while another group given training in large-muscle activities and visual training improved in these attributes but not in reading.[59] I have not found any well-controlled research which supports the supposition that Kephart-type activities enable groups of children to function better academically. It is probable, however, that individual children with movement problems will benefit in specific and general ways from the type of perceptual-motor training outlined by Kephart in his several publications. However, more research concerning these methodologies is certainly called for; particularly studies in which the influences of various components of Kephart's perceptual-motor training program upon the attributes of retardates are investigated.

Despite the scholarly deficits inherent in their theories, their writings have to a great extent encouraged educators and parents to observe and to attempt to remedy some of the obvious motor deficiencies seen in children. The practices outlined by Kephart, in particular, have proved helpful to many attempting to improve the motor functioning of children with minimal neurological handicaps.

Studies of Infant Development. A third type of evidence has been advanced to support the supposition that movement undergirds the intellect. The observation that infants seem to move and to explore their environment with manic-like intensity prior to the emergence of verbal and cognitive behaviors has suggested to some that movement is the base of the pyramid at whose apex stands the higher associative processes.[5, 56]

A survey of the literature in child development, particularly recent investigations of the visual and perceptual behavior of infants during the first weeks of life,[28] suggests that normal infants do seem to learn about some components of their space world through movement. However, the pairing of visual-motor impressions represents only one of the many possible combinations of sensory information the infant uses when collecting data about the world in which he finds himself.

The findings of some investigations suggest that visual discriminations occur prior to the emergence of voluntary movements.[27] Furthermore, the same investigators found that early signs of perceptual activity were more predictive of later psychological development of the child than are the traditional motor measures of infantile intelligence.[27] Numerous other scholars have failed to find that performance scores obtained from two and three year olds are predictive of later intelligence;[3, 7, 11] unless the psychomotor components of such tests are partialed out.[7] Other scholars found that hand-regard in infants was delayed from one to two weeks by enriching the visual surroundings of infants. However, when the infants began to move, even though their movements had been delayed, they engaged in significantly greater amounts of exploratory behavior.[95]

It is probable, according to Kilpatrick that infants organize their perceptions of the world about them in both direct and indirect ways. The infant moves and gains "motor copies" of objects with his exploring hands. With his busy feet, he begins to form impressions of size-distance relationships.[58] As he develops, the child vicariously organizes his environment by glancing briefly at objects and storing the resultant information. He no longer needs direct contact with objects, unless he is afflicted with symptoms of hyperactivity which some perceptually disturbed children manifest. This capacity to learn vicariously about space and space relationships is probably engaged in by children born without arms who never participate in ball throwing and other so-called imperative developmental tasks.[40] Normal children can similarly organize their visual world, without the need for direct motor interaction.

MOVEMENT AND PERCEPTION

A number of excellent laboratory experiments, involving the resolution of visual-motor distortions have produced findings which have been interpreted by some as indicating that movement in imperative to the development of *all* perceptual judgments.[47] However, more of the experimenters involved have taken no such view of their work, and do not generalize to this extent from the findings they have obtained.[48] One series of studies have demonstrated that self-induced movement under the control of the human subjects best resolved various visual distortions of place location produced when grids are inspected through prisms.[47] Passive inspection of such distorting conditions, or when the subjects' limbs were moved by the experimenter as subjects watched their own movements through the prisms, resulted in less accurate responses later.

Studies with animals, kittens and small monkeys similarly point to the importance of self-inspection and self-induced movement in the development of simple visual-motor responses. Kittens in one experiment who were permitted to walk when gaining their first visual experiences engaged in more efficient visual-motor behaviors than did kittens who were able only to see their spatial world without walking through it.[47]

These findings, however, do not offer support for the generalization that movement aids all perceptual processes. Obviously, the cognitive process is important in the organization of the spatial world of children. In the studies of this nature in which animals are used, only very simple visual-motor judgments are required of them. While when human subjects are employed, the investigators seldom include a group who are encouraged to think about the distortion to which they are subjected and then to attempt its resolution.

It is likely that if a group of individuals were added to such studies and were told "the prism makes the grid seem three inches to the left," their performance would approximate that of the subjects who could simply move their hands or their total bodies within the distorting conditions. Indeed the experimenters placed little control over the speed and changes in velocity with which the subjects could make these "self-induced movements," and thus they had no check on the subjects' hypothesis testing at the cognitive level while self-induced movement was engaged in.[47]

The findings of an investigation carried out sixty years ago support the supposition that humans can interpret the nature of visually distorting conditions (inspecting a target through water) to which they are exposed resulting in resolution of the distortion.[55]

Subjects in Kilpatrick's studies were able to resolve the traditional distorted room illusion, when they were able to move a stick or throw a ball around the room or when *they were permitted to watch another individual throw a ball or move the stick.*[58]

Thus, studies in which humans are able to resolve visual-motor distortions to which they are exposed, tell something about the acquisition of specific kinds of motor acts as they are paired with specific perceptual judgments. However, caution should be used in generalizing about such findings, and in attempting to explain the manner in which normal infants organize the totality of their visual judgments.

Factorial studies of visual perception suggest that children and adults evidence several discrete and unrelated attributes. The findings of a study by Smith, for example, demonstrated the existance of several unrelated visual-perceptual traits including the ability to track movements, visual acuity, the ability to fractionalize space (estimate what is one-half between there and here), and the ability to make various size-distance judgments.[86]

Similarly, factorial studies of motor attributes carried out by Fleishman and his colleagues over a period of fifteen years have demonstrated the complexity of the trait structure contained within the totality of motor behavior.[30,31] Therefore, it is inexact to declare that movement, a multi-faceted complexity, positively influences visual perception which is also composed of several separate human attributes. Rather, individuals purporting to aid perception through movement, should delineate the exact perceptual attribute to be modified by specific movement tasks.

MUSCULAR TENSION AND THOUGHT

Some theorists have suggested that the finding that slight muscular tensions accompany thought provides conclusive evidence that there is a motor base to the intellect. Such an assumption, however, is again an over simplification of the relationships involved.

A survey of the literature again provides tentative answers to the relationships between muscular tensions, arousal level, orienting behavior, and learning.[25,79,80,87,18] It is apparent that emotional balance, intellectual ability, and perceptual competence are evidenced by individuals who are capable of *adjusting* their levels of arousal to those appropriate to the tasks confronting them. It is true that muscular tensions frequently accompany intellectual efforts. However, such tensions are merely one of a number of physiological signs that the organism is girding itself for general effort; they do not support the supposition that a causative relationship exists between thought and muscular tension.

There are innumerable investigations supporting the hypothesis that the extent to which a child or adult can control his own activity and arousal level is indicative of good intellectual performance. Studies carried out over thirty years ago found that extra muscular tension, induced in individuals by having them grip hand dynometers, increased their ability to make perceptual discriminations quickly and to memorize work and letter sequences.[80,18,33]

Contemporary studies with retardates and normal children have produced comparable findings. In one investigation, for example, retarded children who were apparently unable, or unwilling, to sit still (measured by means of a force platform imbedded in a chair), were found to be less capable learners than were retardates who remained relatively fixed when seated.[89] Investigators using normal children obtained high correlations between I.Q. scores and those collected when the children were asked to move as slowly as possible in a variety of tasks (walk from here to there as slowly as you can, pull the cart toward yourself slowly, draw a line slowly, etc.)[65] Harrison also designed a study around this principle of arousal control. Subjecting retardates to a program of relaxation training, he found their performance in a number of tasks significantly improved at the completion of the study.[45] One important goal of individuals working with retardates in motor activities should be to help the children to better control their own activity and behavior.

It is possible that periods of self-control for progressively longer time intervals may transfer to the classroom. In that case, a longer attention span, resulting in better orientation to the task, and better learning should take place.*

Thus, delineation of exact parameters must be made when speaking of extraneous muscular tensions and their relationships to thought. There is an optimum level of arousal* necessary for the performance of a given playground or classroom task. The child who is unable to adjust himself to an adequate arousal level frequently has learning difficulties. The child who can control himself, if no other problems are present, uses his intellectual potential more fully and performs better in playground activities.

Zeaman and House have theorized, as the result of a number of experimental studies, that retardation is more likely to be caused by lack of attention to appropriate stimuli than to the inability to discriminate and to otherwise deal with the complexity of the stimuli itself.[99] While other experimenters have taken issue with this simplistic explanation for retardation,[97] it would seem true that some retarded children cannot learn, because they cannot control their attention span. Another portion of the population are unable to learn despite their patient contemplation of each problem with which they are confronted. A third segment of retarded children exhibit excessive motor activity because they are threatened by their perceived ineptitude when confronted with a task that seems too complex.

VISUAL TRAINING

Although the focus of the text is upon motor activity, an ancillary portion of many motor education programs involves visual training. It is difficult to teach

*Studies by the Russian, Sokolov,[87] Luria,[62] and those by Maltzman[66] suggest that a better case may be made for the fact that attention and the orienting "reflex" is the basis for learning than can be made for the role of practice in learning. Studies about infants by Fantz[27] and others, similarly demonstrated the importance of attention in learning. Investigations of this nature have focused both upon the nature of the stimuli eliciting animal and human attention (change in stimuli or novel stimuli) as well as upon the various physiological indices within the perceiving organism which accompany the "what is it reflex."

*Arousal and activation are similar concepts indicative of the appearance of a group of physiological and psychological indices that the organism is preparing itself for some kind of threat and/or intellectual and/or physical activity. Emotional arousal may or may not be accompanied by excesses of muscular tension . . . however, arousal for perceived action and difficulty intellectual efforts are usually accompanied by muscular tension changes in the large trunk muscles.

motor activities without involving a parallel exercise of ocular capacities. As a child watches his own limbs, or tracks the ball thrown to him, his eyes are involved in the activity. Programs of visual training are encouraged primarily by the Optometric Extension Program within the United States. Getman[36, 37] has published a methodology based upon the theoretical speculation that most of what a child learns is acquired through vision. Thus by improving ocular efficiency classroom competence will be directly affected.

It is surprising that, within the many years during which these practices have been engaged in, so few definitive studies have been produced attending to their worth. Inspection of the literature suggests a conflict between findings in which individual subjects have evidenced marked improvement in ocular and accompanying perceptual and academic performance, and data from studies in which group changes are measured after visual-training have been applied en masse.

There seems little doubt that the parameters of ocular efficiency are important to learning. Some tests of visual tracking and of drawing behavior may accurately predict which children entering school may be expected to encounter difficulty learning to spell and to read.[64, 13] While good near-point fusion seems to positively influence reading competency.

Various indices of ocular inefficiencies are sometimes found to be more common among children with reading problems than in populations of children who read well.[13, 61] However, there is little available evidence to delineate exactly how much ocular malfunction is necessary before reading will be impaired.[61] Some children read well, yet their ability to accommodate, to track, and to otherwise use their visual apparatus may be deficient, while other children with minimal visual problems have learning difficulties.

One rationale sometimes given for the correction of minimal eye deficiencies is that the amount of "energy" wasted in overcoming a minor visual handicap will detract from learning. However, most writers on this subject seem to avoid attempting to objectify this "visual energy."

Several conflicting views regarding ocular difficulties are found in professional literature. Some observers suggest the inaccurate visual movements of the reader, as he scans the page, handicaps his reading and comprehension. Others speculate that a child with cognitive disturbances searches in vain through the written material for understanding,[61] and for this reason his eyes tend to jump irradically from word to word. Smith[84] and others have suggested that the inability of severely disabled readers to fixate in ordinary home and school tasks may be stress related, and is a primary source of variability during tasks involving visual discrimination. These conflicting reports concerning the relationship of ocular malfunction to various academic parameters suggest that with our present state of knowledge, each child with learning disabilities should be given a thorough examination in which the many facets of ocular function and visual perception are evaluated.

Attention within visual-motor programs is often directed toward the purported problem of cross-dominance (hand preference differs from the eye preference in one-eyed tasks). Such programs assume that malfunctioning peripheral ocular processes are of more importance than the central processes in reading with comprehension. Whereas in truth, a strong case can be made for the proposition that reading involves the translation of a visual configuration into a verbal-cognitive symbol. Studies by Belmont and Birch[8] and L. Smith[85] indicate that the incidence of cross-dominance is as prevalent in populations of normal children as in groups of children with learning difficulties. An investigation by Stephen, Cunningham, and Stigler recently found no relationship between cross dominance and reading readiness in kindergarten children.[90] 40 per cent of the people in the United States are left-eyed, while 10 to 15 per cent are left handed, and these are not necessarily the same people.[41] Currently, the so-called problem of cross dominance is eliciting less concern among well-informed clinicians.

Efficient tracking behavior may not be a critical quality underlying reading as studies dating from the 1870's indicate that the eyes of a reader more in starts and jerks from word to word, and they are fixed from 70 to 90 per cent of the time as a child reads.[92] Good ocular control is probably necessary to bring the eyes to a stop at places on pages at which the reader desires to look.[61] Recent investigations indicate that when difficulty in reading a word, or in understanding its meaning, is experienced by a child, his eyes make micromovements as they cover the visual pattern (letter or word) which confuse him.[84] Reading, similar to the other processes discussed in these pages, is more complicated than some proponents of visual-motor training suggest. Reading is not dependent solely upon the ability to smoothly move the eyes from side to side. Reading proficiency requires the efficient interaction of several processes including form recognition, the ability to translate a series of word symbols into concepts.

The causes for poor reading are probably as numerous as the causes of retardation itself, estimated to be from 70 to 80. Severe ocular malfunction undoubtedly will prevent a child from engaging in the initial components of the reading process. However, there are other parts in the chain of events described which, if deficient, may impede a child's ability to translate the written page into terms meaningful to him.

The failure to establish hand preference has been cited by some as critical to blocking the intellectual process. However, a survey of the literature reveals that animals at all points on the evolutionary scale evidence asymmetrical paw, claw, and leg use.[41] A grasshopper's preferred leg must be removed before it will begin to scratch with the other one. Rats, evidencing paw preference, could not be trained out of that preference in a study conducted in 1930.[73] Therefore, it is not surprising to find a human evidencing a variety of asymmetrical functions as he walks, uses his upper limbs, and his eyes.

While it is true that children with learning problems often have difficulty establishing a hand preference, it is similarly true that they adopt inefficient work methods when attempting to engage in most of life's activities. Despite the lack of evidence to support importance of establishing hand preference, it is also true that when a child is confronted with a unilateral task such as writing, it is appropriate for educators to evaluate and discover his preferred hand. Specific techniques for accomplishing this are outlined in Chapter 6.

3

SUMMARY

This review of the literature, dealing with relationships to be found among perception, motion, and academic achievement suggest the following conclusions.

1. Movement activities will aid a child to think to that extent to which he thinks about the sequence, variety of categories, and the nature of the movements in which he is engaged.

2. Motor tasks may aid in the development of certain perceptual attributes. Visual-motor coordination is important to accurate hand movement for writing and drawing. In new experiences, if a child is able to handle an object he sees, his tactile sense will support the visual image he received of its size, shape, and texture. The organization of knowledge about objects in distance space may depend upon his past experience and judgments formulated about the size, shape, and texture of objects in near space.

3. Improved motor task proficiency, reflected in improved fitness and sport skills, may result in the increased academic performance of a retarded child whose self-concept has suffered because he has perceived his deficiency in these kinds of motor tasks.

4. Movement experiences may help some hyperactive retarded children reduce the amount of activity they evidence and thereby increase attention span. This self-control may lead toward increased competency in academic tasks.

5. Visual training may aid some children to learn better if a careful visual examination precedes such training and if the components of the training program are applied to the remediation of the specific deficits identified in such an evaluation.

6. Structured movement programs of creeping and crawling are of questionable value in the remediation of anything but locomotor ineptitude.

7. The identification of children with potential learning problems may be accomplished with measures of drawing behavior, scores obtained from measures of balance and other indices of gross coordination, together with an evaluation of visual attributes.

Primary conflicts between observed changes in individual children and the findings of research studies in which group change is surveyed are reconcilable. In the future, studies in which individual differences in the components of the populations studied are identified, would be more helpful than continued investigations of largely undefined populations of children to whom general labels are attached.

REFERENCES

1. Abercrombie, M. J., Gardiner, P. A., Hanson, E., Jockheere, J., Lindon, R. L., Solomon, G., and Tyson, M. C.: "Visual Perceptual and Visuomotor Impairment in Physically Handicapped Children," *Percept. & Mot. Skills,* (Monograph Supplement), *3,* 18, 1964.

2. American Academy of Pediatrics Executive Board Statement: "Doman-Delacato Treatment of Neurologically Handicapped Children," AAP News Letter; 11–16, Dec., 1965.

3. Anderson, J. E.: "The Limitations of Infant and Pre-School Tests in the Measurement of Intelligence," *J. Psychol.; 8,* 351–379, 1939.

4. Ausubel, David P.: "A Critique of Piaget's Theory of the Ontogenesis of Motor Behavior," *J. Genet. Psychol.; 109,* 119–122, 1966.

5. Ayres, Jean A.: "Interrelation of Perception, Function, and Treatment," *American Physical Therapy Association,* 46–47, July, 1966.

6. Balow, I., and Balow, B.: "Lateral Dominance and Reading Achievement in the Second Grade," *Am. Ed. Res. J.; I,* 139–143, 1964.

7. Bayley, N.: "Consistency and Variability in the Growth of Intelligence From Birth to Eighteen Years," *J. Genet. Psychol.; 75,* 96, 1965.

8. Belmont, L. and Birch, H.: "Lateral Dominance, Lateral Awareness and Reading Disability," *Child Development; 36,* 57–71, 1965.

9. Brown, Roscoe C.: "The Effect of a Perceptual-Motor Education Program on Perceptual-Motor Skills and Reading Readiness," Speech presented at research section, AAHPER Convention, St. Louis, Missouri, April 1, 1968.

10. Carlson, Paul V. and Greenspoon, Morton K.: "The Uses and Abuses of Visual Training for Children With Perceptual Motor Learning Problems," Summary of a paper presented to the California Optometric Association Meeting, San Francisco, Feb., 1967.

11. Cattel, P.: "Constant Changes in the Stanford-Binet, I.Q.; *J. Ed. Psychol.; 22,* 544–550, 1931.

12. Cavanaugh, M. C. *et al.:* "Prediction from the Cattel Infant Intelligence Scale," *J. Consult. Psychol. 21,* 33–37, 1957.

13. Chang, T. M. C. and Chang, V. A. C.: "Relation of Visual-Motor Skill and Reading Achievement in Primary-Grade Pupils of Superior Ability," *Percept. & Mot. Skills; 24,* 51–53, 1967.

14. Clausen, Johs.: *Ability Structure and Subgroups in Mental Retardation,* Spartan Books, Washington, D.C., 1966.

15. Cole, J.: "Paw Preference in Cats Related to Hand Preference in Animals and Man," *J. of Comp. and Physio. Psychol.; 48,* 137–145, 1955.

16. Cohen, Abraham: "Hand Preference and Developmental Status of Infants," *J. Gen Psychol.; 108,* 337–345, 1966.

17. Corder, W. D.: "Effects of Physical Education on the Intellectual, Physical, and Social Development of Educable Mentally Retarded Boys," Unpublished special project, Nashville, Tennessee, George Peabody College, 1965.

18. Courts, F. A.: "Relation Between Experimentally Induced Muscular Tension and Memorization," *J. Exp. Psychol.; 25,* 107, 235–256, 1939.

19. Cratty, Bryant J.: *Movement Behavior and Motor Learning;* 2nd Ed., Philadelphia, Lea & Febiger, 1967.

20. ———: *Developmental Sequences of Perceptual-Motor Tasks and Movement Activities for Neurological Handicapped and Retarded Children and Youth;* Educational Activities, Inc. Freeport, L.I., New York, 1967.

21. ———: *The Perceptual-Motor Attributes of Mentally Retarded Children and Youth;* Los Angeles County Mental Retardation Services Board, August, 1966.

22. Davis, R. A.: *Psychology of Learning,* New York, McGraw-Hill Book Co., 1935.

23. Delacato, Carl H.: *The Treatment and Prevention of Reading Problems;* Springfield, Charles C Thomas, 1959.

24. ———: *The Diagnosis and Treatment of Speech and Reading Problems;* Springfield, Charles C Thomas, 1963.

25. Duffy, E.: "The Psychological Significance of the Concept of Arousal or 'Activation'," *Psychol. Rev.; 64,* 265–275, 1957.

26. Fait, H. F. and Kupferes, H. J.: "A Study of Two Motor Achievement Tests And Their

Implications in Planning Physical Education Activities for the Mentally Retarded,'' *Am. J. Ment. Defic.; 60–64,* 729–732, April, 1956.

27. Fantz, Robert L.: ''The Origin of Form Perception,'' *Sci. Am.; 204,* 459–475, 1961.
28. ———: ''Pattern Discrimination and Selective Attention as Determinants of Perceptual Development from Birth,'' in *Perceptual Development in Children,* Aline H. Kidd and Jeanne L. Rivoire, (Eds.) New York, International Universities Press, Inc., 1966.
29. Finch, G. ''Chimpanzee Handedness,'' *Science, 94,* 117–118, 1941.
30. Fleishman, Edwin A. and Ellison, Gaylor, D.: ''A Factor Analysis of Fine Manipulative Tests,'' *J. Applied Psychol.; 46,* 95–105, 1962.
31. Fleishman, Edwin A., Thomas, Paul, and Munroe, Philip: ''The Dimensions of Physical Fitness—A Factor Analysis of Speed Flexibility, Balance and Coordination Tests,'' Technical Report No. 3, The Office of Naval Research, Department of Psychology, Yale University, September, 1961.
32. Francis, R. J., and Rarick, G. L.: ''Motor Characteristics of the Mentally Retarded,'' U.S. Office of Education Cooperative Research Project No. 152 (6432), University of Wisconsin, September 16, 1967.
33. Freeman, G. L.: ''Changes in Tonus During Complete and Interrupted Mental Work,'' *J. Gen Psychol.; 4,* 309–334, 1930.
34. Gagne, Robert M. (Ed.): *Learning and Individual Differences,* Columbus, Ohio, Charles E. Merrill Books, Inc. 1967.
35. Getman, G. N.: ''How to Develop Your Child's Intelligence,'' Luverne, Minnesota, G. N. Getman, 1962.
36. Getman, G. N.; and Kane, Elmer R.: *The Physiology of Readiness,* Minneapolis, Minnesota, Programs to Accelerate School Success, 1963.
37. ———: ''The Physiology of Readiness Experiment,'' Minneapolis; P.A.S.S. Inc., Programs to Accelerate School Success, 1963.
38. Glass, Gene V. and Robbins, Melvin P.: ''A Critique on the Role of Neurological Organization in Reading Performance,'' *Read. Res. Quart.; 3,* 5–52, 1967.
39. Gorelick, Molly C.: ''The Effectiveness of Visual Form Training in a Prereading Program:, *J. Ed. Res.; 57–58,* 315–318, March, 1965.
40. Guarin-Decarie T.: ''The Mental and Educational Development of Thalidomide Children,'' Inter-Clinic Information Service, Committee of Prosthetic Research and Development, Jan. 1968.
41. Hecaen, Henry, and Ajuriaguerra, Julian De: *Left-Handedness Manual Superiority and Cerebral Dominance,* translated by Eric Ponder, New York, Grune & Straton, 1964.
42. Haring, Norris G. and Stables, Jeanne Marie: ''The Effect of Gross Motor Development on Visual Perception and Hand-Eye Coordination,'' *Am. Phys. Therapy Assn. 42–46,* 129–135, Feb., 1966.
43. Harris, A. J.; ''What About Special Theories of Teaching Remedial Reading?'' Current Issues Program, Boston, Mass., International Reading Association Convention, April, 1968.
44. Harris, Charles S.: ''Perceptual Adaptation to Inverted Reversal and Displaced Vision,'' *Psychol. Rev. 72–76,* 419–444, 1954.
45. Harrison, W., Lecrone, H. Temerlin, M. K., and Trousdale, W., ''The Effect of Music and Exercise Upon the Self-Help Skills of Non-Verbal Retardates, *Am. J. Ment. Defic.; 71–72,* 279–282, 1966.
46. Harrington, S. M. J., and Durrell, D. D.: ''Mental Maturity Versus Perception Abilities in Primary Reading,'' *J. Ed. Psychol.; 46,* 375–380, 1955.
47. Held, Richard: ''Plasticity in Sensory-Motor Systems,'' *Sci. Am.; 1–9,* 213–215, 1965.
48. Held, Richard and Mikaelian, H.: ''Motor-Sensory Feedback Versus Need in Adaptation to Rearrangement,'' *Percept. & Mot. Skills; 18,* 685–688, 1964.

49. Howard, I. B., and Templeton, W. B.: *Human Spatial Orientation,* New York, John Wiley and Sons, 1966.
50. Ismail, A. H. and Gruber, J. J.: *Motor Aptitude and Intellectual Performance,* Columbus, Ohio, Charles E. Merrill, 1968.
51. Javel, E.: "Essai sur la physiologie de la lecture," *Annu.— 'Oculist'; 81,* 61–73, 1879.
52. Johnson, G. O. R.: "A Study of the Social Position of Mentally Handicapped Children in the Regular Grades," *Am. J. Ment. Defic.; 55,* 60–89, 1950.
53. Johnson, P. W.: "The Relation of Certain Anomalies of Vision and Lateral Dominance to Reading Disability," *Mono. Soc. Res. Child Dev.; 7-2,* 1942.
54. Jones, M. H., Dayton, G. O., Didon, L. V. and Leton, D. A.: Reading Readiness Studies: Suspect First Graders," *Percept. & Mot. Skills; 23,* 103–112, 1966.
55. Judd, C. H.: "The Relationship of Special Training to General Intelligence," *Ed. Rev.; 26,* 28–42, 1908.
56. Kephart, Newell C.: "Perceptual-Motor Aspects of Learning Disabilities," *Except. Child., 31–34,* 201–206, 1964.
57. Kershner, John R.: "Doman-Delacato's Theory of Neurological Organization Applied with Retarded Children," *Except. Child;* 441–450, 1968.
58. Kilpatrick, F. P.: "Two Processes in Perceptual Learning," *J. Exp. Psychol.; 47,* 362–370, 1954.
59. LaPray, M. and Ross, R.; "Auditory and Visual-Perceptual Training," in *Vistas in Reading,* Ed. J. Allen Figural, International Reading Association Conference Proceedings, XI, 530–32, 1966.
60. Leighton, J. M., Cupp, A. Prince, D. Philabaum, G. McLarren: "The Effect of a Physical Fitness Development Program on Self-concept, Mental Age, and Job Proficiency in the Mentally Retarded." *J. of Physio. and Ment. Rehab. 20,* 4–11, 1966.
61. Leton, Donald A.: "Visual-Motor Capacities and Coular Efficiency in Reading," *Percept. & Mot. Skills; 15,* 407–432, 1962.
62. Luria, A. R., and Vinogradova, Olga S.: "An Objective Investigation of the Dynamics of Semantic Systems," *Br. J. Psychol.; 50,* 89–105, 1959.
63. Lynn, R.: *Attention, Arousal and the Orientation Reaction,* New York, Pergamon Press, 1966.
64. Lyons, C. V. and Lyons, Emily B.: "The Power of Visual Training, as Measured in Factors of Intelligence," *J. Am. Optometric Assn.;* 255–262, Dec., 1954.
65. Maccoby, Eleanor E., Dowley, Edith, M., and Hagen, John W.: "Activity Level and Intellectual Functioning In Normal Pre-School Children," *Child Devel.; 36,* 761–769, 1965.
66. Maltzman, I, and Rasking, D. C.: "Effects of Individual Differences in the Orienting Reflex on Conditioning and Complex Processes," *J. Exp. Res. Personal.: I,* 1–16, 1965.
67. Mosston, Muska: *Teaching Physical Education,* Columbus, Ohio, Charles E. Merrill Books, Inc., 1966.
68. Neale, Marie, D.: "The Effects of a Broad 'Art' and Movement Program Upon a Group of 'Trainable' Retarded Children," International Copenhagen Congress on the Scientific Study of Mental Retardation, Denmark, 7–14, 1964.
69. Oliver, J. N.: "The Effect of Physical Conditioning Exercises and Activities on the Mental Characteristics of Educationally Sub-Normal Boys," *Br. J. Ed. Psychol.; 28,* 155–165, June, 1958.
70. Orton, Samuel Torrey: *Reading, Writing and Speech Problems in Children,* New York, W. W. Norton Co., Inc., 1937.
71. Park, G. E.: "Reading Difficulty (Dyslexia) from the Opthalmic Point of View," *Am. J. Ophthalmol.; 31,* 28–34, 1948.
72. Peterson, G. M.: "Mechanisms of Handedness in the Rat," *Comp. Monograph; 9,* 1–67, 1934.

73. Peterson, G. M.: "Transfer in Handedness in the Rat from Forced Practice," *J. Comp. Physiol. Psychol.; 44,* 184–190, 1951.

74. Piaget, Jean and Inhelder, Barbel: *The Child's Conception of Space,* London, Toutledge and Keagan Paul, 1963.

75. Radler, D. H.: "Visual Training Hopeful-Now Johnny Can Read," *Horizon; 3,* 13–18, 1956.

76. Robbins, Melvyn P.: "A Study of the Validity of Delacato's Theory of Neurological Organization," *Except. Child; 32,* 523–617, April 17, 1966.

77. ———: "The Delacato Interpretation of Neurological Organization," *Except. Child.; 32,* 523–617, April 17, 1966.

78. ———: "Letter to the Editor," *Except. Child.; 33,* 200–201, November, 1966.

79. Semmel, M. I.: "Arousal Theory and Vigilance Behavior of Educable Mentally Retarded and Average Children," *Am. J. Ment. Defic.; 70,* 38–47, 1965.

80. Shaw, W. A.: "Facilitating Effects of Induced Tension Upon the Perception Span for Digits," *J. Exp. Psychol.; 51,* 113, 117, 1956.

81. Singer, G. and Day, R. H.: "The Effects of Special Judgements on the Perceptual Aftereffects Resulting from Prismatically Transformed Vision," *Aust. J. Psychol.; 18–1,* 1966.

82. Singer, Robert N. and Brink, J. W.: "Relation of Perceptual-Motor Ability and Intellectual Ability in Elementary School Children," *Percept. & Mot. Skills; 24,* 967–970, 1967.

83. Smith, C. and Keogh, B.: "The Group Bender Gestalt as a Reading Readiness Screening Instrument," *Percept. & Mot. Skills; 15,* 639–645, 1962.

84. Smith, D. E. P. and Semmelroth C.: "Micro-Movements During Apparent Fixations in Reading, *Yearbook of Nat'l Reading Conference,* U. of Michigan, 3, 4; 188–194, 1964–65.

85. Smith, L.: "A Study of Laterality Characteristics of Retarded Readers and Reading Achievers," *J. Exp. Ed.; 18,* 321–329, 1950.

86. Smith, O. W. and Smith, Patricia C.: "Developmental Studies of Spatial Judgements by Children and Adults," *Percept. & Mot. Skills; 22,* 3–73, 1966.

87. Sokolov, E. N.: "Neuronal Models and the Orienting Reflex," In *The Central Nervous System and Behavior,* Mary A. B. Brazier (Ed.), New York, Josiah Macy, Jr. Foundation, 187–276, 1960.

88. Solomon, A., and Prangle, R.: "Demonstrations of Physical Fitness Improvement in the EMR, *Except. Child; 33,* 177–181, November, 1967.

89. Start, K. B.: "The Influence of Subjectively Assessed Games Ability on Gain in Motor Performance After Mental Practice," *J. Genet. Psychol.; 67,* 169–173, 1962.

90. Stephens, W. E., Cunningham, E., and Stigler, B. J.: "Reading Readiness and Eye Hand Preference Patterns in First Grade Children," *Except. Child; 30,* 481–488, March, 1967.

91. Thompson, M. E.: "A Study of Reliabilities of Selected Gross Muscular Coordination Test Items," *Human Resources Res. Cen. Res. Bull.;* 52–59, 1952.

92. Tinker, M. A.: "The Study of Eye Movements in Reading," *Psychol. Bull.; 43,* 93–120, 1946.

93. Tsai, L. and Maurer, S.: "Right Handedness in White Rats," *Science; 74,* 436–438, 1930.

94. Whilden, Peggy P.: "Comparison of Two Methods of Teaching Beginning Basketball," *Res. Quart.; 27,* 235–242, 1956.

95. White, Burton L. and Held, Richard: "Plasticity of Sensory-motor Development in the Human Infant," *The Causes of Behavior: Readings in Child Development and Educational Psychology;* Judy F. Rosenblith, and Wesley Allin-Smith (Eds.), Boston, Allyn & Bacon Inc., 1966.

96. Whitsell, Leon J.: "Delacato's 'Neurological Organization'; A Medical Appraisal," *California School Health, 3,* 1–13, Fall, 1967.

97. Wickens, Delos D. "The Orienting Reflex and Attention" in *Learning and Individual Differences,* Gagne, R. M. (Ed.), Merrill International Psychology Series, Columbus, Ohio, 1967.

98. Wischner, George J.: "Individual Differences in Retardate Learning," Learning and Individual Differences, Robert M. Gagne, (Ed.), Columbus, Ohio, Charles E. Merrill Books, Inc., 1967. 193–213.

99. Zeaman, D. and Orlando, R.: "The Role of Attention in Retardate Discrimination Learning," *Handbook of Mental Deficiency,* N. R. Ellis (Ed.), New York, McGraw-Hill Book Co., 159–223, 1963.

3

Movement Attributes and Performance Capacities in Infants and Children

In order to evaluate a child who is suspected of possessing various perceptual-motor problems, an understanding should be obtained of the perceptual-motor attributes connected with movement which *normally* may be expected as a child matures. The primary purpose of this chapter is to present a summary of when certain observable behaviors appear during the initial years of a child's life. The final portion of the chapter contains norms of more exact performance measures to which retarded children's performance may be compared.

Several considerations should be kept in mind when reviewing the following material. An individual child may evidence motor attributes which are at variance with the accepted norms, and still be considered a "normal" child. His inability to perform as expected may simply indicate that he needs more experience in a given type of activity, or special help which will enable him to overcome the gap between his performance and the suggested norms. Not only may a child evidence behavior different from that expected, but also he may regress in his ability to perform efficiently a given task or a group of tasks as he matures. When evaluating a child, several variables may influence scores: (*a*). The presence of an observer may upset the child; (*b*) the child may be distracted by the objects he must use; (*c*) the child's momentary level of excitation and/or the presence of a model to be imitated may create problems for him. Thus, indices of a child's perceptual-motor maturation do not always appear in the neat sequences sometimes outlined in the child development literature.

It must be remembered that any theoretical time sequence that lists the emergence of various behaviors does not necessarily describe the development of an individual child.

Any number of factors may contribute to individual differences: (*a*) the presence of an observer may upset the child; (*b*) the child may be distracted by the numerous objects he must use; (c) the child's momentary level of excitation and/or the presence of a model to be imitated may create problems for him. Thus, indices of a child's perceptual-motor maturation do not always appear in the neat sequences sometimes outlined in child development texts.

However, if a child evidences marked delay in developing a specific movement attribute, he should be given a complete physical and psychological assessment as well as an evaluation of his perceptual-motor processes. When the nature of his problems are identified, remediation should be carried out.

MOVEMENT ATTRIBUTES

Body-Image. Some specialists do not consider accurate verbal identifications of body-parts as a "movement attribute" and indeed they are not. There are several kinds of close relationships, however, between the body-image (evaluated by direct responses to verbal directions to move in various ways, or to touch various body parts) and movement itself. Frequently, a close correlation exists between measures of body-image and scores obtained on motor ability tests.[5] Consistent findings indicate that movement activities enhance measurable aspects of the body-image.[9] Very often children with movement problems evidence a concomitant inability to identify accurately body parts, left-right dimensions of the body, and to make similar judgments. Thus, programs in perceptual-motor education frequently have activities which purport to enhance various measurable aspects of the body-image. The sequences were obtained from research by Ilg and Ames,[10] Belmont and Birch,[2] and in studies carried out by the author[5] and his students.

To many, the concept of body-image is a global one, encompassing the totality of percepts, concepts, and feelings formed about the body. Attempts to evaluate the body-image have resulted in requesting children: (a) to verbally identify body parts;[3] (b) to imitate the gestures of an experimenter;[4] (c) to construct a mannequin;[1] (d) to draw a person.[10]

Although a single measure of the body-image has yet to be developed which will satisfy all theorists interested in this elusive concept, the following norms are based upon responses to verbal requests to move in various ways, and to point to various body parts. Admittedly, these data may be primarily a measure of vocabulary rather than an accurate assessment of percepts concerning the body itself. Chart 1 contains three "channels" involving: (a) verbal identification of larger body-parts; (b) verbal identification of hands; (c) identification of various left-right dimensions of the body with related left-right judgments.

Dealing with Objects. Within the first few hours of birth, an infant may be distracted by an object. Within the first weeks, he will begin to watch his hand, and by the third month, he may begin to swipe and to corral objects. Later, this inaccurate behavior will become more refined as he manipulates objects with his hands and mouth. Manipulative behavior is an important channel through which children gain information about their world. The following sequence recorded in Chart 2 was obtained by inspection of the work of Uzgiris,[16] Halverson[8] Piaget,[13] Gesell,[7] White and Held,[17] and others.

Consulting a sequence of this nature should not only provide guidelines for

Chart 1

AGE (In years)	VERBAL IDENTIFICATION OF BODY PARTS	THE HANDS	THE LEFT AND RIGHT
0		watches hands move	
1			
	stomach, head, parts of face, limbs.	identifies hands, fingers, toes	
2			
3			
	objects in relationship to body planes, *i.e.*, "things are in front, back, to the side of me."	identifies thumb little finger, first finger.	knows words "right" and "left", but not that they are on opposite sides of body.
4			
5	shoulders, elbows, knees	identifies middle and ring finger	knows right and left are on opposite sides, but is unable to tell which is which
6	trunk appears in drawings; thighs, forearms, etc. identified		some left-right judgments made accurately
7	wrists, ankles, shins, parts of limbs identified		more left-right judgments on self and in letters, numbers, etc. made correctly
8			can identify the left and right of other people when facing them.
9			can describe the left-right movement of others while watching them
10			

Chart 2

AGE (In Months)	SELECTED BEHAVIORS
1–3	Looks at objects.
2–4	Beginning control of one and/or both arms.
2–4	Arm-waving and other indices of excitation when in the presence of persons and/or objects.
2–4	Examines hand for prolonged periods of time.
2–4	Alternately examines hand and then the object present.
2–4	Corrals objects placed on surfaces in front of him; swipes at objects placed overhead.
2–4	Inspects both hands simultaneously in front of face.
3–5	Slowly brings hand to objects and touches them, alternately glancing at object and hand in the process.
3–5	Hand preference emerges.
5–8	Grasps objects with crude grip, using palms and all fingers placed together.
5–12	Brings objects to mouth for examination by lips, tongue, and inner mouth surfaces.
6–9	Grasps objects with fingers, examines things tactually.
6–+	Exploits objects: hits, stacks, shakes them, begins to let go of objects using crude forms of throwing.
7–+	Begins to search for objects which drop out of view.
10–+	Shows objects to others to instigate social behavior and to get a response.
16–+	Names objects and begins to classify them.

Chart 3

Throwing and Catching Form

AGE (In years-months)	THROWING	CATCHING
2-3	Stiff-arm movement of arm from front to back without body movement.	Stops rolling ball, able to catch large ball but with stiff elbows.
3.6-5	Shift of body weight toward throw.	Elbows in front of body with hands in vice-like position.
5.6-6	Step forward with foot on same side as throwing arm.	
6.6+	Step forward with foot opposite to that of throwing arm.	Mature catching pattern with elbows at the side of the body.

evaluation, but at the same time should suggest helpful training sequences for children with severe movement problems. The sequence is initiated by behaviors which involve orienting reactions to the presence of objects, and to the child's hand itself. The progression of the sequence terminates with behaviors which denote the emergence of conceptualization on the part of the maturing child, including the integration of verbal and social behavior with manipulative acts.

Chart 4

Throwing and Catching, Selected Performance Measures

AGE (In years)	CATCHING (5 trials)	THROWING DISTANCE (In feet)
2	2 out of 5	4-5
3	3 out of 5	6-7
4	4 out of 5	8-9
5	5 out of 5	10-11
6		14-17

Throwing and Catching.   Two theories are advanced for the emergence of throwing behavior in children. Some suggest that throwing evolves from a basic motor pattern which was a necessity to the preservation of life on the part of our evolutionary ancestors. A second explanation suggests that throwing occurs accidentally at first, if, when holding an object, a child moves his hand rapidly and centrifical force dislodges the held missile. The resultant movement and sound made as the object strikes something provides the reinforcement needed for additional attempts.

The developmental sequences outlined in Charts 3 and 4 were obtained from research by Wild[18] and others, as well as from summaries by Espenschade and Eckert.[6]

LOCOMOTOR ACTIVITIES

In addition to motor attributes involving the use of the arms, a child may evidence, in varying degrees, proficiencies in the ways in which he used his lower limbs to move his total body through space. Several sequences will be outlined within this section including beginning locomotor behavior such as walking, hopping, and rhythmic hopping, jumping, and the more complex locomotor movements of galloping and skipping.

Behavior Leading to Walking.   The infant is born with a number of birth reflexes, one of which resembles walking. Soon after birth, however, most of these terminate, and only much later does the child evidence the ability to engage in voluntary locomotion. The progression found in Chart 5 was summarized from the studies of Shirley,[14] Gesell,[7] McGraw,[12] and several other authorities.[6, 10]

Chart 5

AGE (In months)	BEHAVIOR
0–1	Raises chin, lateral head movements.
$2\frac{1}{2}$	Pushes up with arms while lying on stomach.
$5\frac{1}{2}$	Sits alone momentarily.
7	Sits alone steadily.
9	Creeps.
$10\frac{1}{2}$	Walks when led, making stepping movements.
13	Stands alone.
$13\frac{1}{2}$–$14\frac{1}{2}$	Walks alone.

Chart 6

Complex Locomotor Activities

AGE (In years-months)	BEHAVIOR
1	May walk sideways or backwards.
2	
2	May walk on tip-toes, able to walk in straight lines.
3	Can walk 1-inch line, for 10 feet without walking off. Walking rate stabilizes (about 170 per minute)
4	Run, stop, start, turn.
5	Skilled running, with proper arm action, galloping.
6	Skipping.

Chart 7

Jumping

AGE (In years-months)	JUMPING BEHAVIOR
1.6	Steps off height with one foot; momentarily suspended in air.
2	Beginning of double take-off.
2.6	Good double take-off.
3	Standing broad jump with minimal arm action.
4.6	Some skill in high jumping; able to clear 10 inch barrier.
5–6	Jumping using arm movements; can broad jump a distance of 30 to 40 inches.

Jumping. The jumping pattern begins with a one-foot take off, followed by a short period when the body is not supported, ending with a landing on the other foot. Jumping from one foot and landing on two feet occurs next, followed by controlled jumps from both feet, with varying degrees of arm involvement, to landings on both feet. These complex movements involve basic attributes of balance, arm-leg coordination, leg muscle power. Thus, the inability to jump well may be caused by deficits of more than one kind.

One test for assessing motor ability requires children to hop alternately from one foot to the other without breaking their rhythmic hopping pattern. A recent study by Keogh and Pedigo[11] contains norms for boys in this type of motor behavior.

Alternate hopping is dependent upon a number of attributes such as: (*a*) dynamic balance; (*b*) the ability to coordinate two sides of the body; (*c*) the ability to transfer a movement pattern from one side to the other; (*d*) the ability to perceive a rhythmic pattern. The three hopping patterns researched by Keogh and Pedigo were 3/3, 2/2, and 3/2. The children were given a visual demonstration of the pattern and they scored a passing grade: (*a*) if they made a smooth transition from one foot to the other with little or no delay; (*b*) if only one foot touched the ground at a time. Two hundred boys were the subjects in this study.

It is apparent that not until they are eight years old can the majority of boys successfully accomplish even one of these kinds of tasks. At the age of six years 90 per cent or more of the boys surveyed were unable to perform the patterns. The most difficult combination for the boys was the unequal sequence (3/2).

Chart 9 combines some of the measures from previous charts. Using these norms, a parent or teacher should be able to make a cursory assessment of selected motor behaviors of children. For more exact assessment measures, refer to the Appendix, page 192.

Chart 8

AGE (In years-months)	PERCENT OF AGE GROUP WHEN SUCCESSFULLY PERFORMING THE HOPPING PATTERNS*		
	3/3	2/2	3/2
6	3%	10%	3%
6.6	23%	16%	7%
7	35%	19%	10%
7.6	48%	38%	18%
8	63%	53%	31%

*Hopping patterns: 3 left/3 right; 2 left/2 right; 3 left/2 right.

Chart 9

The Acquisition of Selected Perceptual-Motor
Attributes in Normal Children*

A Summary

AGE (In years-months)	ATTRIBUTES
0.4	Looks at hand and at objects
1	Stand Alone Walks alone
2	
	Walks on tip-toes
	Jumps and lands on both feet
3	Evidences weight shift in throwing, but with no step into throw Walking speed, and rhythm stabilizes
	Can walk a line accurately for 10 feet
4	Can catch 16 inch playground ball bounced chest-high to him 4 out of 5 times
	Jumps over 10 inch obstacle
5	Can throw 16 inch playground ball from 10 to 11 feet
6	Broad jumps and runs with good arm action
	Accuracy in left-right discriminations of body and in space
	Can gallop and skip
7	Throws, stepping with foot opposite to throwing arm
8	Alternately hops from one foot to the other with no break in rhythmic pattern
	Can make left-right judgments about another person
9	

*The age at which a majority of normal children evidence the behaviors listed.

AVERAGE PERFORMANCES, BY AGE, IN SELECTED PERCEPTUAL-MOTOR TASKS

The second section of this chapter presents performance averages derived from a study which was carried out specifically to provide content for this text. Three hundred sixty-five children, ranging in years from four to twelve, were tested in a battery composed of five categories of tasks: body-image, general agility, balance, interception of balls, and locomotor ability.

The norms for these tasks are presented by age for selected sub-tasks within this total battery. The averages presented offer helpful guidelines for teachers and parents to evaluate the perceptual-motor attributes of children with movement problems, and to identify the deficient attributes.

Exact procedures for administering these sub-tests are to be found in the Appendix (page 192). Separate norms are presented for boys and girls. In general, it is found that tasks for the balance category differentiate between girls of various ages as do the tasks contained in the gross agility category. The category for locomotor agility, on the other hand, contained tests evaluating two independent attributes, one involving locomotor accuracy, and the other simple locomotor abilities without the need for close visual inspection ($r = .44$). The test in the throwing category employs a ball which may be too large for many childrens' hands. The tests apparently evaluated independent attributes (see correlation matrix, and factor analysis, Appendix, page 203); while at the same time each made a substantial contribution to the total battery score.

Care must be taken when interpreting the scores obtained in the body perception category as correct responses in the second level of this category may be made by chance. If it is felt that a child is indeed guessing, this portion of the test should be administered a second time.

The norms for the battery contained in this section are meant to provide guidelines for the evaluation of motor attributes in which the larger muscles of the body are involved. Fine motor coordinations underlying writing may be assessed by reference to the Drawing Behavior material found in Chapter 6.

On the pages which follow, samples of the behavior which relate to the scores indicated are listed. With one exception, after each section are the average scores for a population of children evidencing minimal perceptual-motor problems, obtained in a study completed during the summer of 1966.[5] Averages on these same tests obtained when testing retarded children (Trainables and Educables) may be found in the Appendix, page 201–202.

Body Perception. Detailed instructions for the administration of the body-perception test are found in the Appendix, page 192. Essentially, the child is to demonstrate that he knows where his front, side, and back are, by lying on them when asked to do so. If a child has a mental age above seven, the initial four parts of the test should be omitted, and only the final part of the test should be administered. The final task involves demonstrating that the child knows what "nearest" something is (lie down with your feet nearest me), and then a series of tasks involving left-right discrimination are given, *i.e.,* lie on your left side, (while in a back lying position) "raise your left hand in the air", "raise your left leg", and finally two tasks in which the child is asked to react to more complex directions, and cross his body, touching . . . ". . . your left elbow with your right hand . . .",

4

Chart 10

Average Scores for 365 Normal Children

AGE (In years)	BEHAVIOR SCORES
4–5	Able to complete first five tasks successfully but unable to make any left-right judgments of body parts better than would be expected by chance.
6	Able to identify accurately left, right arms and legs, but unable to cross body and make complex judgments in final two tasks.
7–11	Children able to make all judgments.

and finally "touch your right knee with your left hand." Achievement scores for a population of 365 normal children are given in Chart 10.

Correlation of the scores of the total subjects in this test to the total battery score was $+.73$.

GROSS AGILITY

The second category involves the agility to move the body in a coordinated manner, while remaining relatively fixed. Two sub-tasks are scored. The first involves scoring how fast a child can arise from a back-lying position, using both

Chart 11

AGE	BEHAVIOR
5–8	Could identify planes of the body, front, back, etc., but no left-right identifications better than would be expected by chance.
9–10	Could not identify left and right better than would be expected by chance.
11–12	Could identify left and right hands, etc., but could not cross body, i.e., "touch your left knee with your right hand."
13–16	Could identify left and right, and could make about one-half of judgments requiring movements across the body, i.e., "touch left elbow with right hand."

Chart 12

Gross Agility Scores for Normal Boys*

AGE (In years-months)	AVERAGE SCORES (In years)
4.6	8.5
5.6	9.5
6.6–11.6	9.75

time and form as criteria. The second involves the duplication of a demonstrated four-count movement from standing position, to kneeling, and back to standing: (1) kneel, (2) kneel, (3) stand, (4) stand. The gross agility score is a combination of scores achieved on each of these two tasks. (See Appendix, page 192.)

The average scores achieved in the gross agility category by normal subjects are given in Charts 12 and 13. In general, the boys' scores clustered so closely, they were not helpful in differentiating between the various age groups. A possible reason for this may rest with measures used in the test, especially the first one which depends upon leg and trunk power, as well as integrative mechanisms. The mean scores for the girls, when plotted by age, however, show a gradual increase. Thus, the score seems more helpful in rating the girls than in differentiating

Chart 13

Gross Agility Scores for Normal Girls

AGE (In years-months)	AVERAGE SCORES (In years)
5	4.75
5.6–6.6	8.45
7.6	8.75
8.6	9.25
9.6–11.6	9.75

*See scoring methods and test administration in Appendix.

between maturational levels of performance for normal boys. (See Appendix, page 199 for norms.)

The same tasks were given to a population of children having a range from minimal to moderate perceptual-motor problems. In Chart 14, the mean scores by age represent the combined scores for the boys and girls.

The difference is apparent between the scores achieved by the normal population and those with motor problems. Thus, this test would seem to be a helpful measure to use in differentiating children with motor problems from those who have no neuromuscular problems.

Correlation between gross agility score and total battery score was $+.48$.

BALANCE

The balance test involves a measure of static balance, evaluated by imposing various stresses upon a child who is asked to posture in an immobile position on one foot. Portions of the test are timed, and, in addition, the child is asked to stand with arms folded, his eyes closed, and finally to posture on his non-preferred foot with the above restrictions imposed. The balance test was found to be the test most predictive of the total battery score in data collected in a previous study using children with minimal to moderate perceptual motor problems ($r = .82$).

Chart 15 represents the average scores achieved by a population of normal children. The scores are separated by sex, when sex differences were significant in the data.

This same test was administered to children with mild to moderate perceptual-motor problems. Again the performance scores for the normal population differed significantly from those of the children with motor problems. In Chart 16, the scores for the boys and girls are combined.

Chart 14

Combined Scores for Boys and Girls in Gross Agility

(POPULATION RANGE—FROM MINIMAL TO MODERATE PERCEPTUAL-MOTOR PROBLEMS)

AGE (In years)	AVERAGE SCORE (In years)
5–8	2.63
9–10	5.9
11–12	8.6
13–16	8.5

Chart 15

Balance Scores for Normal Population of Boys and Girls

AVERAGE SCORE AND AGE (In years-months)	SEX	BEHAVIOR
4.6–5	Girls	Could balance on preferred foot with arms folded for 3 to 4 seconds, eyes open, but seldom for 10 seconds.
4.6–5	Boys	Could balance on preferred foot with arms folded for 10 seconds; unable to balance on preferred foot with eyes closed for 5 seconds.
5.6–6	Girls	Could balance on preferred foot with eyes open for 10 seconds.
5.6–6	Boys	Could balance on preferred foot with eyes closed, and assisted by arms for 5 seconds.
6.6–7	Girls	Could balance on preferred foot with eyes closed and assisted by arms for 5 seconds.
6.6–7	Boys	Could balance on preferred foot with eyes closed, arms folded, for 5 seconds.
7.6–8.6	Boys and Girls	Able to balance on preferred foot with arms folded for 5 seconds.
9–11.6	Boys and Girls	Able to posture on non-preferred foot assisted by arms, with eyes closed, for 5 seconds.

Chart 16

Balance Scores for 38 Boys and Girls with Motor Problems

AGE (In years)	SEX	BEHAVIOR
5–8	Boys and Girls	Could balance on preferred foot, eyes open, using arms for 2 to 6 seconds.
9–10	Boys and Girls	Could balance on preferred foot, eyes open, using arms for 5 seconds.
11–16	Boys and Girls	Could balance on preferred foot, eyes closed, arms folded, for 5 seconds.

Chart 17

Locomotor Agility for Normal Population

AGE (In years-months)	SEX	AVERAGE SCORES
4.6–5	Girls	Able to perform the five tasks but not with accuracy within the squares.
4.6–5	Boys	Able to crawl, walk, jump forward; unable to jump backward or to hop for three consecutive times.
5.6–6.6	Girls	Able to jump forward with accuracy into the squares; had difficulty jumping diagonally into alternate squares in each row; unable to hop or jump backwards with accuracy into the squares.
5.6–6	Boys	Able to execute the five tasks; had difficulty performing the tasks with accuracy into the squares.
7–7.6	Girls	Able to jump accurately diagonally into alternate squares in each row; had difficulty jumping backward with accuracy into the squares.
6.6–8	Boys	Able to jump accurately diagonally into alternate squares in each row; unable to jump backward with accuracy into the squares.
8.6–11.6	Boys and Girls	Able to hop in a row of six squares; had difficulty hopping diagonally into alternate squares in each row.

Chart 18

Locomotor Agility for Population with Perceptual-Motor Problems

AGE (In years)	SEX		AVERAGE SCORE
5.0–8.0	Boys and Girls	3	Unable to jump or to hop; accuracy factor was not used.
9.0–16.0	Boys and Girls	7	Able to jump in a row of six squares; unable to jump diagonally into alternate squares.

The differences between normal performance and the performance of children with motor problems is apparent.

LOCOMOTOR ABILITY

The first level tasks within this category involve: crawling, walking, hopping, and jumping forward and backward three or more times. If the subject completes the five tasks, using the coordination essential to performing the tasks, his total score is 5, 1 for each task.

The second level tasks require a child to jump and then hop with accuracy into twelve squares (1 x 1 foot) inscribed on a mat. There are six squares in each of two parallel rows.

Chart 17 records the average scores by age and sex of the normal population surveyed.

The same locomotor agility test was administered to a population of children with minimal perceptual-motor problems. Chart 18 records the combined scores of the boys and girls in this group.

Correlation between gross agility score and total battery score was +.48.

Intercepting Balls. This test consists of two sub-tasks: the first requires the child to catch a 16 inch playground ball, bounced once from a distance of 15 feet away, so that it rebounds chest-high to the child. The score for this is one point for each of the 5 trials. The second sub-test requires the child to touch with his index finger a softball swung on a string (15 inches long) in a 180 degree arc, at arms distance away from the subject. The ball must be touched before it swings three times. The score is one point for each of the five trials. The score for the total test is 10 points.

Correlation between ball tracking score and total battery was +.81.

A critical time in a child's life occurs when he is five and ready for kindergarten. As he begins school, he should be evaluated to discover, as early as possible, any deficits he may have in his perceptual-motor skills.

Based on the data described in this chapter, several criteria are suggested as a guide to evaluating four-, five-and seven-year-old children. If deficits are discovered, a child should be referred to specialists for a thorough evaluation, so that a remedial program can be given him. Preventive measures are of greater value to the child than applying corrective measures after inaccurate behavior has formed.

SUMMARY

The norms contained in this chapter may be used in a number of ways. The exact performance attributes in a group of retarded children may be measured by using the battery of tests described in the Appendix. At the same time, a less precise check-list of motor abilities may be devised by consulting the material in this chapter, enabling the expeditious survey of a large population of retarded children within a relatively short period of time.

It has been attempted within this chapter and in the chapter discussing drawing and scribbling to present a selection of norms and tests from which the

Chart 19

Ball Interception for Normal Population

AGE (In years-months)	SEX	SCORES
4.6–5	Girls	Caught ball 2 out of 5 trials; unable to touch swinging ball.
4.6–5	Boys	Caught ball 2 out of 5 trials; unable to touch swinging ball.
5.6–6	Boys and Girls	Caught ball _____ trials; unable to touch swinging ball.
6.6–7	Boys and Girls	Caught ball 5 out of 5 trials; able to touch swinging ball 2 out of 5 trials.
7.6–8	Girls	Caught ball 5 out of 5 trials; able to touch swinging ball 3 out of 5 trials.
7.6–11.5	Boys	Caught ball 5 out of 5 trials; able to touch swinging ball.3 out of 5 trials.
8.6–11.5	Girls	Caught ball 5 out of 5 trials; able to touch swinging ball 4 out of 5 trials.

Chart 20

Evaluation Criteria for a Four-Year-Old Child

A four-year-old child should be able to:

1. Walk perfectly, changing speed, and evidence a consistent walking speed and rhythm.
2. Balance on one foot with eyes open for 4 seconds or more.
3. Take three jumping steps forward.
4. Jump off a 2 foot high obstacle, and broad jump 2 feet forward from a standing position.
5. Throw a small ball 10 to 15 feet.

Chart 21

Evaluation Criteria for a Five-Year-Old Child

A five-year-old child should be able to:

1. Balance on his preferred foot, with eyes open, with arms folded, for at least four seconds.
2. Catch a 16 inch rubber ball bounced chest high from distance of 15 feet, 4 out of 5 times.
3. Jump forward and to hop forward on one foot three consecutive times.
4. Identify body parts, limbs, front, back and sides.
5. Run in a coordinated manner, with integration of arms and legs.
6. Jump over a 10 inch high barrier.

It is *unlikely* that a five-year-old will be able to:

1. Identify his left and right body parts better than would be expected by chance (*i.e.*, better than 75% correct responses).
2. Alternately hop from foot to foot, without undue hesitation or placing both feet on the ground simultaneously, in either a 1/2, 3/3, or 2/3 pattern.
3. Touch a ball swinging on a 15 inch string through a 180 degree arc, arms distance away.
4. Jump or hop with accuracy into small squares.
5. Skip.

teacher, parent, or administrator may select according to their needs. Furthermore, certain attributes are indicative of a number of gross motor attributes, and thus additional time may be saved if only they are utilized. For example, the balance test described is highly correlated with a number of gross motor attributes including agility and the like.

CHART 22

Evaluation Criteria for A Seven-Year-Old Child

By the time a seven-year-old child is in second grade, he should be able to:

1. Make all types of left-right identifications of his body parts, body movements, and body-to-object relationships (place the box nearest your left side).
2. Throw a ball with proper step (*i.e.*, using foot opposite to his throwing arm) and weight shift.
3. Get up from a back lying position to a standing position in from 1 to $1\frac{1}{2}$ seconds.
4. Balance on one foot with eyes closed for 5 seconds.
5. Skip, gallop, and run in a coordinated manner (frequently cultural expectations will "corrupt" this performance . . . *i.e.*, girls prefer to skip, while boys prefer to gallop; they may resist skipping).

It is also considered advisable if the measures of gross body agility contained in this chapter are combined with others assessing fine motor ability. Thus the reader should consult the norms for writing and drawing behavior presented in Chapter 6 when devising a battery of tests with which to survey a group of retarded children.

REFERENCES

1. Adams, N. and Caldwell, W.: "The Children's Somatic Apperception Test," *J. Genet. Psych.: 68:* 43–57, 1963.
2. Belmont, L. and Brich, H. G.: "Lateral Dominance and Left-Right Awareness In Normal Children," *Child. Dev.: 34:* 257–270, 1963.
3. Benton, Arthur L.: *Right-Left Discrimination and Finger Localization,* New York, Hoeber, 14, 1959.
4. Berges, J. and Lezine, L.: *The Imitation of Gestures,* (translated by Arthur H. Parmelee) The Spastics Society Medical Education and Information Unit Association, London, William Heinemann, Medical Books Ltd., 1965.
5. Cratty, Bryant J.: *The Perceptual-Motor Attributes of Mentally Retarded Children and Youth,* (Monograph), Los Angeles County Mental Retardation Services Board, 1966.
6. Espenschaɑe, Anna S. and Eckert, Helen M.: *Motor Development,* Columbus, Ohio, Charles E. Merrill Books, Inc., 1967.
7. Gesell, A. and Thompson, H.: *Infant Behavior: Its Genesis and Growth,* New York, McGraw-Hill Book Co., 1934.
8. Halverson, H. M.: "An Experimental Study of Prehension In Infants By Means of Systematic Cinema Records," *Gent. Psych. Mono.: 10:* 107–286, 1931.
9. Hill, S. D., McCullum, A. A. and Sceau, A.: "Relation of Training in Motor Activity to Development of Left-Right Directionality in Mentally Retarded Children: Exploratory Study," *Percept. & Mot. Skills: 24:* 363–366, 1967.
10. Ilg, Frances L. and Ames, Louise Bates: *School Readiness,* New York, Harper & Row, 1965.
11. Keogh, Jack F. and Pedigo, P.: "An Evaluation of Performance On Rhythmic Hopping Patterns," Sponsored by the National Institute of Child Health and Human Development (Grant HD 09059-03), UCLA, 1967. (Unpublished).
12. McGraw, Myrtle B.: *The Neuromuscular Maturation of the Human Infant,* New York, Hafner Publishing Co., 1966.
13. Piaget, J.: *The Origins of Intelligence in Children,* New York: International University Press, 103–107, 1952.
14. Shirley, M. M.: *The First Two Years: A Study of Twenty-Five Babies. Vol. I. Postural and Locomotor Development,* Minneapolis, University of Minnesota Press, 1931.
15. Swenson, C. H.: "Empirical Evaluation of Human Figure Drawings," *Psychol. Bull.: 54:* 431–466, 1954.
16. Uzgiris, Ina C.: "Ordinality in the Development of Schemas For Relating To Objects, In *Exceptional Infant Vol. 1,* Jerome Hellmuth (Ed.), Washington: Special Child Publications, 315–334, 1967.
17. White, Burton L. and Held, Richard: "Plasticity of Sensori-motor Development in the Human Infant," In *The Causes of Behavior: Readings in Child Development and Educational Psychology,* Judy F. Rosenblith and Wesley Allinsmith (Eds.), Boston: Allyn & Bacon, 1966.
18. Wild, Monica R.: "The Behavior Pattern of Throwing and Some Observations Concerning Its Course of Development in Children," *Res. Quart.: 9-3:* 20–24, 1938.

4

Principles of Teaching Motor Skill to Retarded Children

By definition, a retarded child is one who has learning problems. While some writers have suggested that motor ability is one facet of a retardate's personality which more nearly approximates the attributes seen in normal children, little data are forthcoming to support such an hypothesis. While it is true that the motor skill of some retarded children will surpass the skill of the inept normal child, research by Holman and others has shown that to improve the motor performance of retardates on even the simplest of skills, to levels approaching those of normals, extensive practice is needed by the former.[18, 17]

The fact that motor learning is impeded in groups of retardates stems from three primary factors. They usually do not devise efficient work methods when performing and learning motor tasks. Their ability to learn is impeded because of an inability to integrate sensory information well; cues indigenous to the task and cues provided by the instructor.[29] There is a greater likelihood of concomitant neurological impairment in groups of retardates, negatively influencing motor coordination.

It is thus apparent that modifications in teaching methods, as well as adjustments in task demands be incorporated into lessons in which it is hoped to teach retardates motor skills. When teaching skills to retardates, special attention should be given: to teaching for transfer; to conditions which will produce the best retention; to the type of teaching cues employed; and to the nature of the learning environment provided. The techniques which will motivate the retarded child, as he attempts to learn motor skills, should be carefully considered, as well as the length and spacing of the practice periods. The principles suggested in this chapter, which arise from research, provide guidelines for the teaching of motor skills to retardates.

GENERAL CONSIDERATIONS

Important in the teaching of retardates is the clear grasp on the part of the teacher of what perceptual-motor attributes are evidenced at what ages by normal children. For example, Belmont and Birch[2] and others have found that left-right

45

awareness in *normal* children does not stabilize until the age of seven. Thus, to attempt to teach this kind of discrimination to retarded children with lower mental ages should only result in frustration to the retarded child and to their ambitious teachers.

There are several evaluative instruments which may be applied to retardates,[7,9] as well as of assessment instruments with which the motor functioning of atypical groups of retarded children may be described. Garfield, for example, has devised simple scales with which various self-care and motor functionings of retarded children with cerebral palsy may be measured.[12] A more detailed presentation of sub-scales describing perceptual-motor sequences through which normal children pass as they mature was found in Chapter 3.

In general, it would seem that children, in order to develop to their optimum, need visual-motor-tactual experiences during the early months of life. The findings of several studies demonstrated that children with learning difficulties who had been reared in institutions, usually were less capable than those who had been home reared. Thus, hypothetically, it would seem that retarded babies need a great deal of verbal, visual, and motor stimulation if they are to develop their potential.

At the same time, the necessity for vocational preparation demands that a continuing program of motor skill acquisition should be a part of the total educational program of the more capable retarded children as they reach late childhood and adolescence. In addition to early stimulation and preparation for a vocation, successful participation in playground skills should enhance the retardate's social skills and general self-confidence. Movement of the total body in space can be formed into a helpful learning channel as described in Chapter 11 which discusses learning games.

It is axiomatic that the quickest learning, and thus the most satisfying learning, occurs when a child is taught a skill using the whole method rather than the part method. Difficulties do occur, however, when attempts are made to determine just what constitutes the total skill. Invariably, consideration of the capability of the learner must be referred to when attempting to define "wholeness." When teaching skills to retardates, the whole skill for normal learners frequently needs to be broken into parts. At the same time, interest in the activity will lag among retardates, just as it will among normals, if too small a portion of the skill is taught at a time. In essence, it is advisable to expose a retardate to as large a portion of a given skill (or the total skill) as he can organize.[16]

THE TEACHING ENVIRONMENT

Distractability is a characteristic of many retarded children. It is essential to provide a distraction-free environment when attempting to teach motor skills. Too often the teacher leaves the classroom because she feels she must use the playground, when exposing retarded children to movement experiences. Actually, the more restricted but less distractive confines of a corner in the classroom may be the best place of all for skill development, providing it has the necessary equipment.

Learning activities for severely retarded young children must not be structured within too large a space. Their attention will wander, and they will fail to focus upon the teacher and the activities she provides if a large playground is used for all big muscle activities.

Thus, the distraction of the environment and the size of the space in which motor activity takes place are two important considerations. The research in motor learning contains many studies which indicate the disrupting effect disturbing conditions have upon skill performance.[4] In a program I administer it is found that motor training for some hyperactive retardates was best accomplished in indoor handball courts. At times, a highly disorganized child is placed in this room with only his instructor because children distract each other. After such a child has accommodated to the demands of a simple task (or tasks) for a period of time, the learning conditions are gradually made more complex as one or two additional children are added to the group.

For optimum skill development, the teacher should attempt to manipulate the size of the environment, the number of extraneous stimuli present, as well as the number of children within a group. As the child seems able, the group size may be increased gradually, and the number of distracting objects, persons, and things may be increased.

The information contained in Chart 23 is meant to provide general guidelines. Accurate recommendations are not possible without weighing several parameters such as: (a) the make-up of the teacher's personality, (b) the nature of the facilities, (c) the emotional stability of the children, (d) the quality of previous associations between teacher and child, (e) the available equipment and other similar facets of the environment.

Chart 23

Approximate Class Size and Space Size Recommended for the Teaching of Motor Activities to Retarded Children

AGES	I.Q. RANGE	MAXIMUM GROUP SIZE	MAXIMUM SPACE RECOMMENDED
2–6	Untestable–54	4–6	15 x 15 feet
2–6	55–80	4–6	20 x 20 feet
7–10	Untestable–54	6–8	30 x 30 feet
7–10	55–80	8–10	100 x 100 feet
11–15	Untestable–54	10–12	30 x 30 feet
11–15	55–80	10–16	100 x 100 feet or larger for base games
16–20	Untestable–54	10–12	50 x 50 feet
16–20	55–80	10–20	limited by activity needs

It is believed unrealistic to expect a teacher of physical education to accomplish anything constructive with retarded children with a teacher-pupil ratio less favorable than that enjoyed by the classroom teacher. The grouping together large groups of retarded children for physical activities lends itself to little but a mass program of teacher-directed exercises.

TEACHING CUES

Three basic considerations are important when formulating the nature of the sensory information to be used in teaching retardates: (a) the nature of the sensory-input: tactual, verbal, visual, kinesthetic, olfactory; (b) the speed with which this type of information is given to the child; and (c) the intensity of the stimulus.

It is often suggested that to learn best, one should attempt to incorporate all types of sensory information into the learning process. Care must be exercised, however, when applying these simplistic principles to the teacher of skills to the retardate. Generally, the "channel capacity" of the retarded child is limited; and while he may be able to learn after hearing verbal information, seeing a demonstration, or being manually guided through the movements of a given skill, it is unlikely that he can really organize more than one type of input at a time.

Several principles govern the teaching of skills to a normal population relative to the nature of sensory information afforded; several other principles apply to the teaching of retardates. During the initial stages of learning the task, information from an instructor has the greatest effect if cues concerning the general spatial requirements of the task and mechanical principles involved are extended to the learner. Information concerning the exact way in which movements in the task are made is generally more effectively extended during the early stages of learning. The initial elimination of errors is better than attempting to later correct an "ingrained" mistake.

While in normal children verbal communication is important to learning, when teaching skills to retarded children, it is usually more helpful to depend upon visual information and upon manual guidance. Care should be taken, however, when showing a film depicting a skill, or when demonstrating a skill, that the movement be mirrored, *i.e.,* faced in the same way as the learner is faced. If a manual skill is demonstrated, the teacher should reach over the child's shoulders (assuming he is seated) and engage in the skill using the same hands in the same way as the child will be expected to perform. If manual guidance is the next step, this should be given in the same way—his hands should be guided by reaching around him, with the teacher standing to his rear, if possible. A visual demonstration may have a positive effect upon the skill-learning of retardates because many of them have exceptionally good visual memories.[26]

Emphasis should be placed, particularly during the initial stages, on the acquisition of effective work methods because it is in devising ways to do a task that the retardate lays the groundwork for later success or failure. He needs specific information how to arrange himself relative to the task, how to lay out materials, what to pick up first, and exactly how to hold an object in a construction task. He needs to be told to look at his hand when he is drawing, and whom he should watch when playing a game.

In research carried out in 1966, I found that if retardates were asked to stand on one leg, many did poorly, because they simply did not know how to position their body over the foot remaining on the ground, rather than because they had a balance problem. When some were instructed later to "place their body over the foot staying on the ground" with an accompanying push in the required direction, their scores improved remarkably. Frequently, a retardate's attention will stray from his hand as he attempts to draw. If this occurs, his efforts will improve, not by adjusting the nature of the drawing task, but simply by instructing him in the proper work method, *i.e.,* "watch your hand".

The timing of the insertion of teaching cues into the learning process is critical in the skill-learning of retardates. Physical education instructors of normal children and young adults sometimes "over-teach" to a remarkable degree.

It is imperative that a minimum of cues be given to retardates, and that these bits of information about the task be properly spaced in time. It is not unusual to observe a rather lengthy response delay in retardates, similar to that seen in a normal two- or three-year-old child. A retardate may listen and look, and then take several seconds or longer (a minute or more) to process the information, decide upon some action, or decide upon inaction. If, during the time interval the child is using to process this information, the teacher directs additional cues his way, confusion is likely to occur. These second bits of information are likely to create "psychological noise" within the retardate's "learning circuits," interfering with the prior information he is attempting to process. Therefore, for best results when teaching skills to retardates, the teacher should wait patiently, allowing for this "processing time", and not pile confusion on confusion by pressuring his students with too much information too rapidly.

LEARNING SCHEDULES

A frequently researched phenomenon in learning has been termed reminiscence, which is the improvement of skill because of spaced practice. Innumerable studies have been carried out exploring the best ratio of rest-to-practice time in order to elicit best learning. When practice trials are arranged too close together, a condition known as response inhibition builds up. In this state, less and less improvement is noted from trial to trial as the learner seems to become bored with the task at hand and manifests less motivation. It is also true that as learning in a given task progresses, the learner hypothetically approaches his physical and/or psychological limits; thus, further improvement is difficult, if not impossible, simply because of the nature of his neuromotor make-up.

Generally it is found that if a task is interesting to the learner because of what motivates him or the inherent novelty and complexity of the task, this response inhibition is less likely to be seen when inspecting the learning curve. When performing such a task, the learner continues to improve even though practice periods may be spaced closely together in time.

Taking these together, (*i.e.,* inhibition, task interest, and reminiscence), it becomes apparent that, at times, a task, whose simplicity might bore an average learner, continues to offer a challenge to a retardate. The latter, therefore, will continue to improve with massed practice, evidencing little of the boredom or response inhibition that would be likely evidenced if the learning curve of a normal learner were inspected.[4, 28]

Thus, when instructing retardates in big and small muscle activities, the teacher should be sensitive to several primary principles. Initially, he should mass practice until he observes symptoms of boredom on the part of his charges, and then he needs to space his practice. The teacher should realize that his own boredom with the simplicities of a task may not be felt by the students; in fact, they may be willing to continue, and to improve, even though the practice trials are closely spaced in time.

Recent evidence suggests that the absolute time between trials of a task is not as important in the production of better learning as the ratio between practice time and resting time. If a practice session lasts for a prolonged period, it seems better, according to available information, to permit a rather lengthy period of time between practice sessions.[25] On the other hand, if practice is brief, a brief rest period may suffice.

The teacher should realize, however, that many motor skills have an optimum length for a practice period, after which time little improvement will be noted in a given day. Freeman, for example, found that practice in writing for fifteen minutes a day was desirable.[11] Additionally, it should be realized that a variety of combinations of practice-rest schedules are possible. One may either space mass or progressively mass or space the practice of a single skill within a given practice session, and/or may evolve some desirable combination of massing or spacing the practice sessions themselves. Thus, even though a given period of time is alloted to motor skill teaching, the instructor has the prerogative of spacing and/or massing practice of a given skill or sub-skill within this practice period.

TEACHING FOR TRANSFER

Coupled with the interest in the spacing and massing of practice has been a parallel interest of experimenters in the nature of transfer of training.[10] Transfer is the effect the learning of one skill has upon the other. It is, therefore, an important consideration when dealing with retardate learning.

Generally, retardates do not transfer experiences very well. An example will illustrate the point. I was guiding a retarded nine-year-old girl as she attempted to learn to ride a bike within a large playground surrounded by a high chain-link fence. As I grew tired toward the end of the session, she pulled away from me for an instant, and crashed, with some discomfort, but no injury, into the fence. This somewhat upset her, but when shortly afterward I again fell behind, the child nearly hit the fence again, but at a different section. Fortunately, I was able to overtake her this second time, and managed to stop her. However, following this second near encounter with the fence, she evidenced no fear because she had been approaching a *different* point in the fence, which apparently did not threaten her. It was only later when she again sped ahead of me that her behavior illustrated how little she was able to transfer an experience, a concept, and a principle. It was *only* when she approached the *same* place in the fence, where she had met with her first accident, that she evidenced fear and agitation. She thus seemed unable to generalize from her first experience the principle that *all* points in the fence, upon being encountered by her bike, could cause discomfort. Rather, she had only learned that hitting the fence in *one specific spot* was potentially injurious.

It is very important to determine the extent to which a retarded child is able to transfer from task to task. Can he learn only task specifics, or can he generalize principles? In several ways a teacher, working in perceptual-motor skills, can increase the type and number of tasks to which a trained-for activity may positively transfer.

In general, transfer to a given task will be more likely if a number of training tasks are used to contribute to the final reference skill or concept to be improved. There seems little doubt that motor activity, in which various one-handed and one-footed movements are emphasized, will contribute to a retardate's awareness of right and left.[15] But the concept of right-left will not necessarily become engrained unless a *number* of right-left things are carried out. Depending upon a single right-left game probably will teach retarded children only that game.

A recent project in which left-right discriminations were asked of retarded children, as they were lying on their backs, revealed that they could play "An-Angel-In-The-Snow-Left-Right-Game" (sliding the correct arm and leg along the mat), but when they arose and were asked for other left-right judgments, they were unable to make judgments of this nature better than would be expected by chance.[7]

If good performance in a sorting task is desired on the part of retarded children, the teacher should attempt to engrain concepts of sorting items according to various qualities possessed by items. In a series of studies by Clarke in England, for example, it was found that concepts relative to sorting were transferable from task to task among retardates, despite the fact that different kinds of discriminations were required by the children.[3]

Stemming from the work by Harlow[14] in 1948, in which it was found that primates and children could transfer various learning "sets" from task to task, interest has focused on the general factors which cause transfer, as opposed to specific motor or stimulus components which may transfer. It is important to instruct children in the reasons for a particular drill, or the principles underlying an exercise, in so far as their levels of understanding permit; for example, just what muscles are being strengthened and why?

If the goal is to improve the self-concept of retarded children by increasing their physical proficiency, then the transfer for this goal must be taught. The children, themselves, must be made aware of the amount and the nature of their improvement. A specific experience will illustrate this point.

In a program in perceptual-motor education which I direct at the University of California at Los Angeles, a pre- and post-test battery, spaced at a five-month interval, was administered to the children. One item of the test, which revealed this lack of transfer, had to do with the children's physical proficiency, and their self-concept of this improvement. While the test scores demonstrated an actual improvement in the children's physical skills, the test scores pertaining to their self-concept of this improvement revealed little or no transfer. They continued to believe they were very poor in their physical skills, yet in reality, they had improved after participating in the program for a five-month period.

In searching for reasons to explain this discrepancy between the child's actual physical improvement and his lack of self-knowledge about his own improvement, it was evident that the activities of the program had failed to teach for transfer.

After testing the *children,* the *parents* were invited to a group meeting at which time the director, using various charts and graphs, demonstrated to the parents the improvement of the children. This meeting served the valuable purpose of communicating to the parents what the program was doing for their children. The parents were most appreciative, but unfortunately, communication stopped at this point. Had this same emphasis been placed on communicating to *the children* in various ways the nature and amount of their own improvement during the entire five-month period, the test results of their self-concept might have reflected a comparable improvement.

If retardates are to learn about the differences in various geometric shapes, by playing on them on a playground, they must be taught in what Clarke has called "conceptual sharpening."[3] If the goal is a lesson on triangles, a child must first learn about triangles tactually, visually, and verbally in a classroom. After the lesson has been taught, the child may be taken to the playground where he is directed to find similarly shaped objects. This kind of cross modal transfer, occurring between sensory modalities, has been researched by Pick and others. It is an effective way to ingrain percepts and concepts in retarded children.[25]

Expecting transfer to occur by chance will usually prove disappointing. Expecting a child to become better able to organize the right and left, or things in space, by making sure he salutes the flag with the correct hand each morning will be as unproductive as expecting him to recognize shapes better by sending him to a playground containing various shapes without accompanying efforts being made to conduct a lesson in geometric shapes.

Another group of research studies has dealt with the problem of how transfer occurs best: (*a*) from a simple task to a complex one; (*b*) from a complex one to a simple one; (*c*) from a simple one to a simple one; or (*d*) from a complex task to a complex task. In general, it is found that more transfer can be expected when transfer *to* a complex task is taught for in some way, either from another complex one, or from simple ones which relate in some way to the more difficult task. A complex task, used in this context, infers that it is a difficult task for a particular learner to master. A young child and a retarded child will find a large number of life's tasks complex; whereas mature and capable individuals will have mastered most of the motor skills in life which are important to them by the time they reach maturity.

It is becoming increasingly evident that studies in which efforts to transfer skill, using subjects who are mature and capable generally produce findings which suggest that no transfer takes place. Indeed, in this case, the transfer has probably happened to the second complex task prior to the time some kind of short-term experiment has been engaged in by the group of subjects. On the other hand in experiments in which retarded and younger normal children have been used as subjects, findings have been produced which suggest that engaging in some kind of related lead-up activity is likely to produce transfer to a variety of skills. It is evident that the experimental conditions have contributed in a real way to the background of these less experienced subjects, and so as to improve their performances in a number of motor skills.[3]

The transfer elicited in these studies probably stems from the acquisition of specific skills and skill components, as well as from the acquisition of general principles arising from related tasks. Methods of spatially organizing visual-motor tasks adjacent to the limbs and eyes, principles of ordering the steps in a construction task in a helpful series, ways of placing parts of an assembly task on the desk in front of the learner, and similar basic principles learned in one task probably transfer positively to other motor skills.

Thus, when teaching both fine and gross motor skills to children, if teachers keep in mind the principles of transfer as outlined above, the children may achieve greater success in a variety of tasks. On the other hand, if teachers focused on a given task and fail to point out to retardates just what principles and generalizations underly the performance of that task, they will find themselves starting from the beginning each time a new skill is to be acquired.

MOTIVATION

Motivation is an often-used term for which each theorist in education seems to have his own definition. The definitions range from the circular, (*i.e.,* motivation is something which is more likely to elicit a given response when a given stimulus appears again) to more general definitions which include psychological and social factors. In general, a motive is something that impels individuals to work harder and longer at a task, and to channel their interests so that they select a given task to perform in the first place!

Motives stem from three general sources: (*a*) factors within the task itself such as its novelty, complexity; (*b*) factors within the individual (psychological and physiological needs of various kinds; and (*c*) factors external to the task and to the individual, including candy and social or monetary rewards. A good case, of course, could be made for the fact that motives within one category trigger those within another. Social approval triggers some kind of psychological need for success, while the sight of candy certainly sets off various physiological responses in children and adults.

A mistake made by many experimenters interested in the study of motivation is repeated by many teachers. At times it is assumed by both teachers and behavioral scientists that what motivates *them* will motivate their *subjects* or students. This assumption is not always true. Retarded children, normal children, and adults often achieve reinforcement for successful performance in a task independent of any obvious rewards extended to them from others.

The findings from Marston's recent study contrasting self-reinforcement, and external reinforcement illustrates this point quite well.[21] One group of subjects took a chip, which later could be exchanged for a prize each time *they* judged *themselves* as accurate in a dart throwing task. A second group was awarded a chip by another person who judged their accuracy in the same task. Upon finding that the self-rewarded group performed in a manner superior to that of the externally rewarded group, Marston concluded that external reinforcers may suspend or otherwise interfere with reinforcers individuals give themselves. He further concluded that reinforcers considered positive by an experimenter actually may have negative effects on subjects.

In considering the use of reinforcements, two important factors must be considered. The type of reward is one factor, but what is equally important is the crucial period during the learning period that the reward is extended. Generally, it is believed that some knowledge of results is imperative for learning, but the knowledge of just how successful one is, in a motor task, will usually elicit improved performance on subsequent trials. When applying the principle of reinforcement to the actual learning process, the sensitive teacher must have insight to spot the strategic moment in the learning process to reinforce.

In studies carried out with normal subjects, it is apparent they know how well they are doing, and they are sensitive to any improvement despite information being given or withheld from them after each trial. In one study I conducted,[8] blindfolded students, running successive trials through large mazes, were equally proficient and inscribed comparable learning curves whether or not they were informed of decreases in traversal speed after each trial. *They* knew they were passing more quickly through the mazes in each trial, whether or not they were told, and this self-knowledge was sufficient to elicit increased efforts on subsequent trials.

The retardate, however, may not have the capacity to make the kind of self-estimate seen in the subjects in the above study, nor of the kind made by normal children. Aarts,[1] for example, found the accuracy of estimates of personality traits, and body size positively related to I.Q. Thus, it may well be that teachers must provide an awareness of increased task proficiency in as exact terms as possible to retarded children upon completion of a given trial, or when parts of a complex task have been mastered.

Timing the knowledge of the results of their activities is critical when working with retarded children. Some delay should be permitted after they have completed a task so the feeling they experience about their improvement may be absorbed by them. These feelings about themselves seem to be more effective than an immediate reward of any kind (*i.e.,* candy, monetary, or social).

The appropriate nature of the reward extended to retardates depends on the nature of the task, the maturity of the learner, and the place of the task in the learning schedule. For example, Gordon *et al.*[13] found that social encouragement was best applied during the initial stages of a motor task performed by retardates involving persistence ("how long can you hold your leg out to the front while seated in a chair"). Appropriate behaviors of severely retarded children in basic self-care skills have been successfully using the principles of reinforcement espoused by Skinner.[27] When attempting to work with severely retarded, hyperactive children, it may be helpful to start by offering rewards for periods of *immobility;* and after this is accomplished, it might then be helpful to reinforce motor behavior of a highly controlled nature (*i.e.,* "how slowly can you walk from here to there") before attempting to teach any stimulating activities of a more complex nature.

Gestures and/or verbal comments are forms of social approval frequently used by children and adults. However, if they are applied too often they tend to lose their reinforcing qualities. If they are used appropriately and sparingly, they will continue their desired effect for a longer period of time.

To an increasing degree, research has focused upon the apparent motivating characteristics that lie within a task. It is apparently satisfying to most people to do well in what is for them a reasonably complex and/or novel task, independent of any monetary reward, social approval, or similar reinforcers.

Principles arising from this research have important implications for the education of retarded children. For it is found that there is an optimum amount of novelty and/or complexity which will elicit the most productive learning and best performance on the part of children and adults. If the colors on the blocks are too garish, anxious children may be frightened by them;[22] similarly, if the blocks are too plain, they will not attend to or manipulate them for any length of time.

However, the degree of novelty and/or complexity which motivates retarded children often differs from the conditions which motivate normal children. If the task or stimulus appears too difficult to the normal child, he will attempt the task because he has a tolerance for ambiguity and frustration. The impaired child, on the other hand, is easily threatened by situations he perceives as too difficult and may tend to withdraw. The normal child, if faced with situations that are easily solved, many times will practice anyway, believing that it may aid him to reach future goals. The retarded youngster usually evidences no such composure. He may be insulted by the simplicity of the task, and again he is likely to leave it.

One difficulty when teaching skills to retarded children is not only a poor tolerance for complexity and simplicity, but the fact that what is novel, complex, and interesting to them today becomes ordinary, too simple, and not worthy of their attention tomorrow. Thus, to achieve optimum performance and learning on the part of retarded children, one must constantly change the nature of the stimulus to which they are exposed.

At times, however, similar responses may be engendered by dissimilar stimuli. If the desired motor skill is accuracy in jumping and hopping behavior, the creative teacher will change the kinds of things the children must look at and jump into or over. For one lesson, the teacher may drop a rope in various configurations on the ground, and encourage the children to react with the correct responses. The next day hoops may be substituted for the rope, and placed on or near the ground. On subsequent days, sticks, tires, and similar equipment or objects may be used to elicit the same jumping and hopping response to the changing visual stimuli.

Such a course of action satisfies the principle of transfer previously outlined. Similarly, these changing stimuli should prove to be more interesting than using the same objects each day. This principle should be used to secure the children's interest and attention in the serial learning problems presented in Chapter 11. If the participating children find the same configurations daily, their interest will soon wane.

It would seem, therefore, that severely retarded children who require a gradual build-up in simple responses and response clusters react very well to the principle of behavioral modification. An excellent starting technique is one in which the offering is immediate and obvious, such as the candy bits. Later, social reinforcement followed by the application of the principles of novelty and complexity of the task offer a logical sequential pattern for molding the behavior of retarded children. With increased competency and maturity, the child will begin to find satisfaction in the mastery of many tasks independent of any obvious external rewards attached to them.

RETENTION

In the absence of definitive studies dealing with the retention of skill in retardates, the one exception, a study by Howe,[18] it might prove helpful to formulate some factors that contribute to the retention of motor skill by normal subjects.

Retention is best if there has been an optimum degree of overlearning based upon some criteria of success. If it is desired that a child throw a ball at a target 5 times out of 5, continuing practice until he can do it about 7 or 8 times perfectly will probably insure his ability to accomplish this task 5 times without error. However, to continue practice until he can perform the task 20 times out of 20 may be wasteful of time. Thus, there is an optimum amount of over-learning which is productive of optimum retention in a given task.[4]

Verbal or motor tasks that are rhythmic in nature, composed of related parts, and have internal consistency, are retained better than those that are not. Thus, motor activities such as folk and popular dances are remembered better by retarded children than the complex and often unrelated rules in a baseball game. Prose is more quickly forgotten than poetry, and nonsense syllables are the most difficult of all to retain.

Tasks whose practice has been interrupted are retained better than tasks that have been finished, and to which the learner has stopped attending. It may be a good practice occasionally to stop a task just before the final step has been learned, so that the participants will be eager to retain the first steps of the task when they confront it on the following day. This has been termed the Ziegarnik effect.

The type of learning schedule such as the massed versus distributed practice is not as predictive of skill retention as are the variables previously discussed. Final levels of learning, of over-learning, of the coherence of the task and its parts are more predictive of retention than the nature of the practice schedule in which the original learning took place.

For the best retention, it is imperative that the retarded be given information before practicing a skill they will be expected to retain. Furthermore, they should be told they will be called upon to perform the skill again, and they should be given the reasons for learning a given skill. Research by Lavery[19] supports the importance of the initial "setting" of learners with the idea they will be expected to retain verbal and movement tasks. The instructions to retain, as well as the instructions the learner brings with him to the learning environment, interact to establish an early attitude toward the learning of a given skill. It is important that the nature of this attitude be a positive one; that the learner is aware of the purpose of the skill; that indeed he will be expected to perform it at some future time. The absence of such instructions to retain a skill result in significantly less retention.

SUMMARY

Upon consideration of the scant experimental literature dealing with the skill-learning of retardates, and studies concerning motor learning in which normal subjects have been used, together with my clinical experiences, I believe the statements below to be valid generalizations relative to the focus of the chapter. Obviously, these statements are subject to revision upon the emergence of new research findings.

1. A general motor development program for low-level retardates need not consist of the variety of activities considered desirable in programs designed for retarded children who are more capable.

2. The presence of distracting stimuli, the size of the area in which the teaching takes place, as well as the number of children in a group are all important considerations when teaching motor skills to retardates. In general, the younger and less capable children should be dealt with in smaller groups, in controlled environments, and in relatively small areas.

3. Initial efforts in the learning situation should concentrate on gaining the attention of the children, of encouraging self-control or teacher control if necessary, and of adjusting their levels of arousal and excitability to those appropriate to the tasks to be learned.

4. The quickest learning occurs if a skill is taught as a whole, or as much of the entire skill as the learner is capable of acquiring. Complex skills should be broken down into parts for easier assimilation.

5. Transfer of training between various skills will occur to the extent to which it is taught by building cognitive bridges between tasks. Common principles should be emphasized when teaching skills which are in any way similar.

6. Transfer to a percept or concept through motor activity or from skill to skill will take place to the extent to which a number of sub-skills, or tasks contribute to the acquisition of the concept.

7. Transfer occurs because of similar response elements in two tasks, because of common principles and work methods common to the two tasks.

8. Teachers of motor skills should be aware of the general order of difficulty of related motor tasks, and of approximate developmental norms appropriate to normal children, so that realistic tasks and expectations are presented to retarded children.

9. Visual demonstration, practice, and manual guidance are generally more appropriate than extensive verbal explanations when attempting to teach skills to retardates. Demonstrations and other instructions are usually more helpful during the initial stages of learning.

10. When teaching retardates motor skills, it is important to engender proper work methods, to aid them with their ''motor planning'', to help them acquire movement patterns involved. Many retardates perform motor tasks poorly because they do not decide upon a proper plan of execution, and not because of basic motor ineptitude.

11. When teaching for transfer to perceptual or conceptual materials, it is helpful if several sensory modalities are utilized. A triangle may be described, looked at, touched, and walked around.

12. Basic learnings of severely retarded children may be helpfully shaped with simple, immediate, and obvious rewards. As the children become more capable, rewards inherent in the nature of the task, its novelty and complexity, as well as social approval assume increasingly important roles.

13. The retardate should be continually supplied by the teacher with information informing him of his general improvement in physical fitness and skill, as well as with immediate information relative to a single improvement in a given task.

14. Retention will be best in skills which are rhythmic and integrated in nature, and in skills which have been overlearned.

15. Retention will be best in skills, when previous to practice, the children have been informed that they must retain the skill, and how the skill is to be used.

REFERENCES

1. Aarts, J. F. M. C.: "Some Experiments On the Accuracy of Self-Judgements," *Arto. Psychol.; 25,* 137–158, 1966.

2. Belmont, L. and Birch, H., "Lateral Dominance, Lateral Awareness, and Reading Disability, *Child Devel.; 36,* 57–71, 1965.

3. Clarke, A. D. B. and Cooper, G. M.: "Age and Perceptual-Motor Transfer in Imbeciles: Task Complexity as a Variable," *Br. J. Psychol.; 57,* 113–119, 1966.

4. Cratty, Bryant J.: *Psychology and Physical Activity,* Englewood Cliffs, New Jersey, Prentice-Hall, Inc., 1968.

5. ———: *Movement Behavior and Motor Learning,* 2nd Ed., Philadelphia, Lea & Febiger, 1967.

6. ———: *Social Dimensions of Physical Activity,* Englewood Cliffs, New Jersey, Prentice-Hall, Inc., 1967.

7. ———: *Perceptual-Motor Attributes of Mentally Retarded Children and Youth* (Monograph), Los Angeles County Mental Retardation Services Board, 1965.

8. ———: "Characteristics of Human Learning In a Locomotor Maze," *Calif. J. Ed. Res.; 14,* 36–42, 1963.

9. Clausen, Johannes: *Ability Structure and Subgroups In Mental Retardation,* Washington, Spartan Books, 1966.

10. Ellis, Henry: *The Transfer of Learning,* New York, The Macmillan Co., 1965.

11. Freeman, Frank W.: "Principles of Method in Teaching Writing as Derived From Scientific Investigation," 18th N.S.S.E., Yearbook, 11–25, 1919.

12. Garfield, Agnes and Shakespeare, Rosemary: "A Psychological and Developmental Study of Mentally Retarded Children With Cerebral Palsy," *Devel. Med. & Child Neur.; 6,* 485–494, October, 1964.

13. Gordon, S., O'Conner, N., and Tizard, J.: "Some Effects of Incentives Upon the Performance of Imbeciles," *Br. J. Psychol.; 45,* 277–287, 1954–55.

14. Harlow, H. F.: "The Formation of Learning Sets," *Psychol. Rev; 56,* 51–65, 1949.

15. Hill, S. D., McCullum, A. A. and Sceau, A.: "Relations of Training in Motor Activity to Development of Left-Right Directionality In Mentally Retarded Children: Exploratory Study," *Percept. & Motor Skills; 24,* 363–366, 1967.

16. Hirsch, William: *Motor Skill Transfer by Trainable Mentally Retarded and Normal Children,* Doctoral Dissertation, UCLA-Education, 1965 (Unpublished).

17. Holman, P.: "The Relationship Between General Mental Development and Manual Dexterity," *Br. J. Psychol.; 23,* 279–283, 1932.

18. Howe, C.: "A Comparison of Motor Skills of Mentally Retarded and Normal Children," *Except. Child,; 25,* 8, 352–354, April, 1959.

19. Lavery, J. J.: "Retention of a Skill Following Training With and Without Instructions to Retain," *Percept. & Mot. Skills; 18,* 275–281, 1964.

20. Malpass, Leslie, F. P.: "Motor Proficiency in Institutionalized and Non-Institutionalized Retarded and Normal Children," *Am. J. Ment. Defic.; 6,* 1012–1015, May, 1960.

21. Marston, Albert: "Self-Reinforcement and External Reinforcement in Visual Motor Learning," *J. Exp. Psychol.; 74,* 1, 93–98, 1967.

22. Mendel, Giseld: "Children's Preferences For Differing Degrees of Novelty," *Child Devel.; 36,* 452–464, 1966.

23. Oxendine, Joseph B.: *Psychology of Motor Learning,* New York, Appleton-Century-Crofts, 1968.

24. Pick, A. D., Pick, Herbert and Thomas, Margaret: "Cross-Model Transfer and Improvement of Form Discrimination," *J. Exp. Child Psychol.; 3,* 279–288, 1966.

25. Plutchik, Robert and Petti, Rodger D.: "Rate of Learning on a Pursuit-Rotor Task At A Constant Work-Rest Ratio With Varying Work and Rest Ratios," *Percept. & Mot. Skills; 19,* 227–231, 1964.

26. Siipola, Elsa M. and Hayden, Susan D.: "Exploring Eidetic Imagery Among Retarded," *Percept. & Mot. Skills; 165,* 21, 275–286.

27. Singer, Robert, N: *Motor Learning and Human Performance; An Application to Physical Education Skills,* New York, The Macmillan Co., 1968.

28. Skinner, B. F.: *The Behavior Of Organisms: An Experimental Analysis,* New York; Appleton-Century-Crofts, 82, 84–87, 91, 93, 98–101, 104, 119, 1938.

29. Tizard, J., and Loos, F. M.: "The Learning of a Spacial Relations Test by Adult Imbeciles," *Am. J. Ment. Defic.,* 1950.

30. Zuckerman, John V.: "Effects of Variations In Commentary Upon The Learning Of Perceptual-Motor Tasks From Sound Motion Pictures," *Psychol.; 5,* 363–364, 1950.

5

The Adjustment of Arousal
Level and the Improvement
of Attention

It is not uncommon to find among retarded children a large number who might be termed hyperactive. It is also true that excessive activity, which overly arouses retarded children, is an impediment to learning. Cognizant of the many subtle problems retarded children manifest, Zeaman and House suggest an obvious one which they consider to be a primary contributing factor to mental retardation. This is the inability of retarded children to focus their attention on any given task.[11]

Their research analyzed the learning curves in visual discriminatory tasks among various groups of retardates. They found the primary factor, which differentiated the I.Q. sub-groups within their population, to be the inability of some children to even begin to focus on the assigned task. The learning curves of the brighter children reflected immediate focus of their attention to the assigned task, whereas the beginning of the learning curves of the less capable children were characterized by prolonged periods of inactivity.

Ounsted similarly found that the I.Q. of hyperactive retardates was lower than that of children who were apparently more self-controlled.[9] In studies carried out with normal children, high correlations have been obtained between I.Q. and scores in tasks in which motor control is called for (i.e., "walk as slowly as you can from here to there").[8] Harrison attempted to determine whether he could exert a causal effect upon learning by incorporating training intended to reduce the arousal level of a group of children. His positive findings suggest that indeed specific kinds of activities designed to help retarded children achieve and maintain self-control would be helpful within educational programs for children with learning difficulties.[2]

Some measures used to evaluate the activity level of children are: direct observation and scoring the duration of time a child is in motion; measuring the amount of free movement within a prescribed area using electronic scoring techniques (pressure plates in the floor, light beams crossing the room); and various "figetometers" in which any slight movement in chairs or while standing on a platform may be recorded.[1,10]

In general it was found that the activity level is, in reality, composed of several factors, and not just one.[1,11] One type of activity is purposeful movement which is related to objects. Other types of hyperactive behavior, head banging and the like, are general types of self-stimulation and are not goal centered.

A number of causes for hyperactivity in children have been postulated. Some research studies suggest the persistence of an immature stage of development during which time the child feels compelled to inspect everything around him. Others have postulated that hyperactivity is a neuromotor "spillover" which is caused by some malfunction in one of the several stages within the perceptual-integration-motor process. A third possible cause has been attributed to the child's selection-rejection system; he may be attempting to handle too many stimuli.[1]

It has also been found that the activity level in people is a function of daily and monthly cycles, and it is influenced by barometric pressure changes. As age increases, the activity level of normal children and of retardates tends to decrease. Laufer found that hyperactivity of retardates decreased between the twenty-fifth to the thirty-fifth year. Increased visual stimulation seems to increase activity, while the appearance of novel, odd, and complex stimuli will often serve to reduce activity and focus attention.[6,10]

But despite theoretical arguments concerning causation and conflicting research findings concerning the effects of various remediation procedures upon hyperactivity, there is universal agreement upon the axiom that a marked lack of control of motor functions accompanies and causes learning problems.

Procedures which hold promise for reducing the purposeless activity of the distractive child are eagerly sought by teachers in special education. A few techniques are offered. They have been used in various research studies,[4] in clinical settings,[3] as well as in classrooms within the Los Angeles City Schools during the past several years. They are not presented as the final answers, but as promising beginnings in the search for activities which may place the hyperactive child under better control. Continued research is needed in this area, and more refined methodologies are needed.

RELAXATION TRAINING

In 1938 a book[3] on progressive relaxation outlined procedures which have undergirded programs carried out during the intervening years by many psychiatrists, doctors of physical medicine, and physical therapists. The methods are intended to aid individuals to relax by making them aware of residual muscular tensions over and above those needed to carry out life's activities. The procedures are designed to help people *consciously* relax by controlling their emotions, thereby preventing some extension of the emotional factors contributing to excess tension.

While it is true that muscular tension does not always reflect psychic upset, at the same time, emotional disturbances, particularly in individuals who habitually tense their muscles under stress, are likely to be reflected in overt muscular activity of a chronic nature.

Case studies of severely disturbed individuals, that were reported in a recent forum dealing with the effects of conscious relaxation, demonstrated significant changes after Jacobson's techniques had been used.[4] The same publication reported that training for relaxation is particularly helpful to children who respond more readily to this type of neuromotor education than the adults do. Many teachers may find this explanation of the techniques helpful to them.

1. The individual or the group should seek as comfortable a position as possible in an environment with all distracting stimuli removed. For example, have the children put their heads on their desks, and let their arms hang limply downward. If mats are available, have the children lie on their backs, arms at the side, and a small roll under the knees, so that the large leg muscles are in a relaxing position.

2. The children should be talked into alternately tensing and then relaxing their total body and/or parts of their body using whatever verbal imagery is appropriate to their intellectual and maturational level (''make your muscles as hard as you can'' . . . ''tighten your stomach'' . . . ''hard . . . harder . . .'' . . . ''clench your fists as tightly as you can'').

3. Efforts should be made: (*a*) to help the child become aware of the *degrees* of tension they can exert by saying "now tighten your muscles one-half that hard" or "now tighten your muscles one-fourth that hard" as he exerts maximum tension for five to eight seconds followed by a relaxation period; (*b*) to help them become aware of unwanted tension in *various parts* of the body. It is helpful, for example, to alternately tense and to relax various muscle groups while moving from the head to the feet, and then up the body again . . . by saying "tighten your jaw . . . harder . . . harder . . . now relax . . . now touch your shoulders . . . now make *them* tight . . . now relax . . . completely . . . make the muscles in your arm . . . tighter . . . now make them as light as you can . . . take all the muscles out of your arms . . . etc.

4. Movement of the relaxed limbs may be carried out to see if the unwanted muscular tensions have been dissipated. The child may be asked to lift his arm over his head, and then let it fall of its own weight to his side or to the mat, if he is in a back lying position.

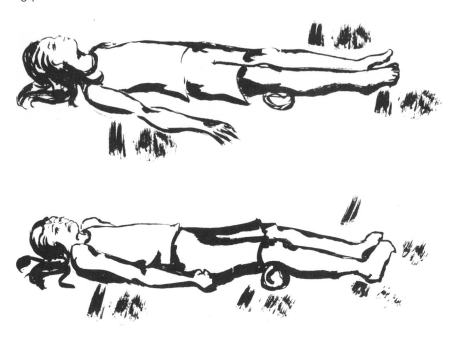

5. Special emphasis should be placed upon the muscles in the face, forehead, neck, and jaw, for it is in these locations that general anxiety accompanied by muscular tension is most often reflected. Neck relaxation exercises are helpful if followed by slow head movements of a rolling nature to test just how much contributing tension has been removed.

6. Various kinds of verbal imagery, of course, must be applied to children with various levels of intellectual ability. Directions to: "Make yourself light . . . and then heavy . . . sink as far as you can into the mat" and similar general and simple directions are appropriate.

7. An effort should be made to help the child focus tension in specific body parts, while relaxing others. For example, he may be directed to tighten one arm only. Then the teacher or a child may test to see if the other arm and legs have remained relatively relaxed.

8. The teacher or a child may want to determine whether a child has been able to direct tension into specific limbs and combinations of limbs when asked to do so. He may be asked to lift one arm, while keeping the other arm and legs relaxed. The child may then be asked to move just his arm; later to move an arm and leg on the same side, while keeping the limbs on the opposite side immobile and/or relaxed. The most difficult task, of course, is to move a limb and leg on opposite sides of the body (left arm and right leg), while keeping the two other body parts immobile. The teacher may make this kind of practice more difficult by asking the children to keep their eyes closed. She may need to hold the limbs, if the object is for the child not to move; she may help the limbs move by holding them, and starting them herself.

Conscious relaxation can be of a general nature by focusing attention upon the ability to direct tension in specific parts of the body, thereby eliminating the neuromotor "spillover" often seen in children with coordination difficulties. Relaxation of this nature should be given after children have been subjected to arousal producing activities (games, exercises vigorously carried out, etc.), and prior to their return to various classroom tasks or manual skills. Such training may result in a program of perceptual-motor education to be followed by other types of activities to be described.

Classes of retarded children, who have experienced lessons in relaxation, are told that if they find themselves becoming too excited to work or becoming upset, they may go to a corner of the room, lie down, and consciously relax.

It is interesting to observe classes becoming aware of excessive tension, which is socially transmitted, *requesting* a relaxation period of their teacher, and then returning to productive work. Hyperactive behavior is not reinforcing to some children; they do not like to be upset, and eagerly accept techniques offered to them for reducing their tensions.

In the program I administer at University of California, Los Angeles for some hyperactive children this kind of training constitutes one-half of their total program. For example, some children engage in agility, balance, and ball-handling activities for one half hour, and the final half hour they lie down in a dark indoor handball court, and learn to relax using the techniques outlined above.

PROLONGING ACTIVITIES

Another type of activity found helpful in aiding a child to gain control of himself is to present motor tasks which may be engaged in for increasingly longer periods of time. The basic assumption underlying this component of the program is, if a teacher can encourage a hyperactive child to do something longer than he has done anything before, his attention span may be prolonged in other tasks as well. Gross and fine motor activities are appropriate tasks for two reasons: (a) they seem to marshall several kinds of sensory stimulation at the same time (visual, kinesthetic, etc.); and (b) prolonged attention or inattention to a motor task is easier to observe than a task involving visual attention only.

One boy in the experimental program at the University entered the program with an attention span from five to eight seconds. After a few months of work, with a single instructor, he was willing and able to engage in a variety of motor tasks for periods of time ranging from three to five minutes. These tasks consisted of walking lines of increasing length, drawing lines through patterns of increasing complexity on a blackboard, and attempting to keep a tennis ball balanced on a board 2 x 2 feet while holding the board in both hands.

A primary principle to keep in mind, when attempting to hold a distracted child's attention, is the need to constantly change the complexity of the task. Otherwise, after frequent exposure to the task, he may perform it while giving relatively little of his attention to it. For example, if a balance beam is gradually lengthened, as the child's skill improves, he may be watching everything around the room while walking the beam. To hold his attention to the task, vary it by placing ropes at intervals across the beams, so that he must "watch his step."

In one experiment, a hyperactive boy was placed on a large wooden rocker and instructed to walk back and forth for increasing periods of time. At first, the task was a challenge and he walked gingerly, but willingly on the unsteady plat-

form. Soon, however, his visual attention was drawn to everything around the room, while at the same time he was meeting the demands of the motor task. Again, to readjust his attention to the task at hand, footprints were painted on the level side of the rocker into which he had to place his feet.

It is apparent that a child may seem to attend to a task while performing it, yet his visual attention, if the task is too easy or if it has been overlearned, may wander to innumerable other components of the environment. The initial attention of a child to a task may be achieved by offering him immediate rewards, knowledge of his results (his scores), and by the difficulty of the task. However, continued attention to the task will be maintained only if it is made increasingly challenging for the child.

Frequently, rewards are given for fast performance in various tasks, but seldom are children rewarded for going as slowly as possible. Yet, this is the kind of reinforcement hyperactive children need. Indeed, they are surprised, and delighted, when they realize they can decelerate themselves, thereby gaining better control over their movements. After they recognize their own capability to control and regulate their movements, the rate of their movements decrease and their accuracy increases.

IMPULSE CONTROL

Closely associated with activities described in the preceding sections are tasks to see just how slowly a child can move. Taken from the research by Maccoby and others,[8] such tasks should consist of those in which the total body is in motion as well as those in which the specific limbs are involved while the body's center of mass may remain fixed.

Thus, a child may be asked to see how slowly he can draw a line across the blackboard or how slowly he can walk a line. Competition may be utilized effectively with some groups of children as three children, starting from a back lying position on a mat, may be asked to see who can "get up last." Thus the winner (the child up first) is the loser!

To some children such restrained movements may be tension producing in themselves. Therefore, it is wise to intersperse some relaxation activity between such tasks. After hyperactive children demonstrate their ability to move very slowly, efforts should be made to see if they can be "turned on." "How fast can you get up?", and then determine if they have good control by an activity such as "How slowly can you do it?"

Line drawing is a good activity for encouraging slow, controlled movement. Children may start from opposite sides of the blackboard, running their chalk down a narrow "road" composed of parallel lines. The child who gets across the board first is the loser!

Impulse control activities of this nature are often effective when accompanied by music to give children an awareness in sensory modality of just what slowness means. Indeed all of the activities described in this chapter are many times more effectively carried out if appropriate music accompanies their application.

GENERAL CONSIDERATIONS

It is impossible to give any specific directions for working with special children because of the many variables surrounding the situation. The weather, some experience on the way to school, the events of the school day, are just a few of the many variables that radically change the levels of arousal on an hourly and/or daily basis, in the normal child, and to a greater degree, in the hyperactive child. However, there are some guidelines for teachers of special children.

Because hyperactivity is a serious impediment to learning, teachers should be free to use any acceptable technique essential to establishing control over the child who lacks control when faced with a learning task. Regulatory activities, for the lethargic child as well as the hyperactive one, cannot be scheduled for a particular time in a specific place. The sensitive teacher must be free to insert activities to counteract any disrupting influence at that time during the day that the needs of a specific child demand.

SUMMARY

Research has demonstrated that lack of attention caused by hyperactivity is a disruptive factor to effective learning for retarded children. Furthermore, there is evidence to demonstrate that specific training in self-control aids hyperactive retarded children to be more productive in the classroom.

Three techniques are recommended to help children gain better control of themselves: (a) conscious relaxation to help children to identify and to deal with disruptive residual muscular tensions; (b) prolonged motor tasks to encourage hyperactive children to engage in motor tasks for longer periods of time, as a means of extending their attention span; and (c) direction of impulse control activities to demonstrate to children they can slow themselves down, and place themselves under better control by learning to move slowly.

It is recommended that activities be used wherever and whenever they appear to be needed by one child or a group of children within a class of retarded children. Further research is needed to refine these suggested techniques.

REFERENCES

1. Cromwell, Rue L., Baumeister, Alfred and Hawkins, William F.: "Research in Activity Level" (Chapter 20, 632–663), In Handbook of Mental Deficiency, Normal R. Ellis (Ed.), New York, McGraw-Hill Book Co., 1963.

2. Harrison, Wade, Lecrone, Harold, Temerlin, M. K. and Trousdale, W.: "The Effect of Music and Exercise Upon the Self Help Skills of Non-Verbal Retardates," Am. J. Ment. Defic.; 71, 2, 279–282, 1966.

3. Jacobson, Edmund: Progressive Relaxation, Chicago, The University of Chicago Press, 1938.

4. ————: Anxiety and Tension Control: A Physiologic Approach, Philadelphia, J. B. Lippincott Co., 1964.

5. Kagan, Jerome: "Body Build and Conceptual Impulsivity in Children," J. Person.; 34, 118–128, 1966.

6. Laufer, M. W., Denhoff, E. and Solomons, G.: "Hyperkinetic Impulse Disorder in Children's Behavior Problems," Psychosom. Med.; 19, 38–49, 1957.

7. McKinney, J. P.: A Multidimensional Study of the Behavior of Severely Retarded Boys, Doctoral Dissertation, Ohio State University, 1961, (Unpublished).

8. Maccoby, Eleanor E., Dowley, Edith M., and Hagen, John W.: "Activity Level and Intellectual Functioning in Normal Pre-School Children," Child Devel.; 36, 761–769, 1965.

9. Ounsted, C.: "Hyperkinetic Syndrome in Epileptic Children," Lancet; 2, 303–311, 1955.

10. Semmel, M. I.: "Arousal Theory and Vigilance Behavior of Educable Mentally Retarded and Average Children," Am. J. Ment. Defic.; 70, 38–47, 1965.

11. Zeaman, David and House, Betty J.: "The Role of Attention In Retardate Discrimination Learning" (Chapter 5, 159–223), Handbook of Mental Deficiency, Norman R. Ellis (Ed.), New York, McGraw-Hill Book Co., 1963.

12. Zeaman, D., House, Betty J., and Orlando, R.: "Use of Special Training Conditions in Visual Discrimination Learning With Imbeciles," Am. J. Ment. Defic.; 63, 453–459, 1958.

6

Scribbling, Drawing and Writing

During the first days of birth, the infant evidences an awareness of movement in space and shortly after that time looks at his own moving hand.[9] It is not until many months later, however, that he gains the ability to hold a writing implement and to demonstrate graphically his awareness of some of the dimensions of space and form. From the time he first looks at objects in space to the time the child acquires writing skill lie several general and many specific sub-skills. Before he can scribble, for example, the child must be able to hold a writing implement with a reasonable degree of facility. Some of the sub-stages in the development of drawing ability include:

1. Attention to a writing implement, hold it, and watching others make marks with it;
2. Crude scribbling seemingly at random, without producing any coherent design;
3. Rudimentary space perception evidenced by coloring within the general outlines of a figure;
4. Ability to stay within a design, and accurate drawing of figures;
5. The reproduction of more complex designs, and drawing pictures of objects.
6. Prints numbers and letters;
7. Acquires handwriting skills, with decreasing amounts of visual monitoring of movements needed, *i.e.*, can write without the need for constantly watching his moving hand.

Kellogg[5] identified five similar steps in the acquisition of hand-control when drawing and writing, including: the scribbling stage, drawing diagrams, combinations of diagrams "combine stage," more complex designs incorporating three or more diagrams "aggregate stage," and the final stage in which pictures are made with varying degrees of accuracy "pictorial stage."

Within each one of these general areas, however, innumerable sub-tasks have been identified by various authors. Kellogg, for example, has named approximately 20 steps within the "scribbling" stage.

Obtaining exact developmental norms for graphic skills of children are difficult because innumerable variables can modify the accuracy of a child's attempts to scribble, draw, and write. For example, whether a child may choose to use a writing implement at all is dependent upon how much of this activity he observes within his home. Culturally deprived children may thus be at a disadvantage in this respect, since their parents, in their struggle for a living, may not have the time to join them in mutual endeavors involving coloring and drawing.

Other environmental supports will also influence the accuracy of a child's drawings. Imitation of another's drawing movements will sometimes produce more accurate attempts than will spontaneous attempts on the part of the child without the presence and/or stimulation of another person.

At the same time the child's accidental movements, as he makes various kinds of marks on a page, may prove self-reinforcing and lead to the pursuance of drawing and refining forms. For example, an accidental spiral or circular movement of the arm, producing a corresponding circle or spiral or series of spirals on a page, will be usually enjoyed by the child. He may then attempt consciously to reproduce the pattern which originally resulted from a chance movement.

Ample educational materials are available which purport to stimulate drawing abilities in children. Essentially two basic principles will aid in selecting the type of material best suited to stimulate a child to draw. One type of activity should permit the child to use his arms, wrists, and hands in free and relaxed movement patterns (have children draw circles on the blackboard using one hand and then using both hands simultaneously). The other idea is to develop the ability of a child to reproduce patterns with some degree of accuracy by tracing around various forms of objects. These ideas and others are developed on pages 90–97.

Other controversies underlie the development of drawing and writing abilities in children. The majority of educators advocate that a child should be encouraged to draw with increasing accuracy within the lines of coloring books and similar tasks, while art educators maintain that too early restriction of a child's attempts to draw will inhibit his creative potential.

On the pages which follow, several facets of children's drawing behaviors will be examined in detail. Initially, the developmental sequences lying within some of the more general areas of maturation presented previously will be outlined. Then, various remedial techniques will be listed and evaluated. The concluding sections of the chapter will deal with the normative data gathered from a study of form drawing which I recently completed together with findings outlining the change which was elicited from children with drawing difficulties after their participation in a perceptual-motor training program.

DEVELOPMENTAL SEQUENCES

The Scribbling Phase. Between the fifteenth and eighteenth months of life, as the child begins to exploit objects in various ways (*i.e.,* throwing, hitting, stacking), he may also begin to imitate scribbling movements by watching another child or adult. Such movements usually begin as simple tentative marks. However, as the child gains more confidence, these scribbling movements become bolder, more repetitive, complex and refined.

His first drawings are shaky lines, horizontal, vertical, or radiating from a central spot.* Within a few weeks, if writing implements continue to be made available, he will begin to draw patterns in which vertical and/or horizontal lines are repeated. This early developmental phase is indicated below:

Initial lines, dots.

Repetitive vertical, radial, and horizontal lines.

By about the eighteenth month, the child may begin to react to forms as he scribbles. Behavior such as that which follows will often be seen:

1. He will tend to "block-out" a form placed on a page, if it is a small one.
2. If the form is large enough (about 6 x 6 inches), the child may begin to scribble reasonably well within its confines.

*Neither information from available research studies, nor the results of clinical observations of children give conclusive evidence concerning whether the tendency to make horizontal, vertical, or lateral lines appears first. It seems that as children *scribble,* the three configurations are likely to appear with about equal probability. However, as children are asked to *draw figures with accuracy,* lateral lines are apparently more difficult.

3. The child may also attempt to balance his scribbling movements on a page by marking on the side of a sheet of paper that is opposite an already present figure. The following illustrates this phenomenon:

Shortly thereafter, usually about the twenty-fourth month, semicircular lines and initial attempts to enclose space will appear. First attempts will be irregular, but later attempts will consist of repetitive loops and spirals. This second phase includes:

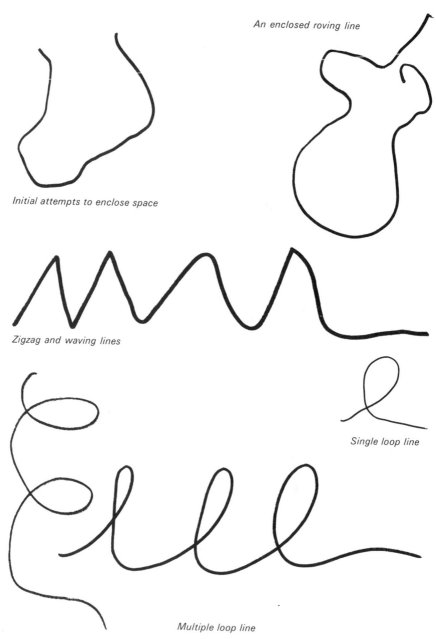

An enclosed roving line

Initial attempts to enclose space

Zigzag and waving lines

Single loop line

Multiple loop line

During these initial attempts, the child may begin to evidence hand prefer-ence, though the hand used will vary from time to time. It is helpful if the parent will observe any preference which emerges during these early attempts at graphic representation. Eberhard[1] has contributed research which indicates that manipula-tive movements are a product of central processes as well as of hand musculature. The "eye-thinking" practice, then, that a child obtains during these early scribbling attempts are as important as the practice obtained by the specific hand em-ployed.

The next phase in the scribbling sequence involves drawing various spiral-shaped movements with the child's hand remaining stationary. If he uses his left hand to draw these spiral shaped movements, usually they are done in a clockwise direction and if he uses his right hand, they are usually done in a counterclockwise direction. Steps within this sequence are:

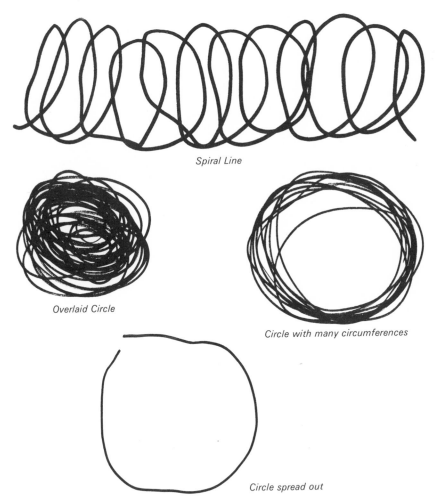

Spiral Line

Overlaid Circle

Circle with many circumferences

Circle spread out

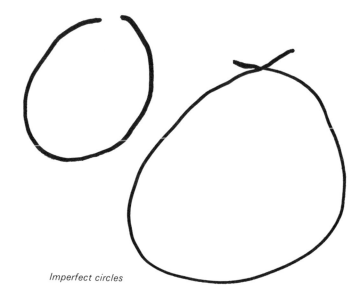

Imperfect circles

The Diagram Phase. The "diagram" phase which occurs next overlaps the "scribbling" stage in time. For example, it is not unusual to find that a child may, during the scribbling stage, accidentally, and later imitatively, form a cross by intersecting two lines, vertical and horizontal. Interesting studies of primate drawing behavior indicate that primates can also reproduce such a primitive diagram.[7] In humans, the first crosses appear as multiple scribbles crossing other multiple scribbles. Here are examples of these early crossing configurations:

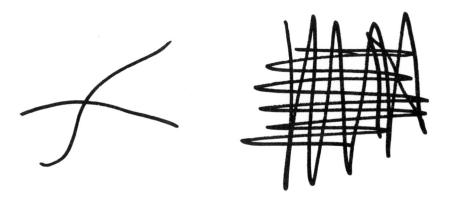

By the age of three, a child can usually reproduce a circle copied from a card. The degree of accuracy with which the child accomplishes this feat is presented in the concluding portion of this chapter.

With the passing of time, squares are produced. Three conditions affect the appearance of the first squares in children's drawings: (*a*) multiple crosses accidentally assume a squarelike pattern; (*b*) circles gradually begin to square off; and/or (*c*) the sides of the paper on which the child is writing is being reacted to. As the child nears the age of four, he can usually copy a square with reasonable accuracy. Steps involved in the ability to copy a square are enumerated below:

(a) Accidental square-making, arising from vertical and horizontal line drawing and cross-making.

(b) Squaring off circles.

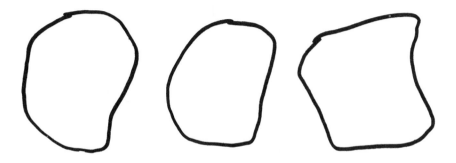

(c) Reaction to the sides of the paper.

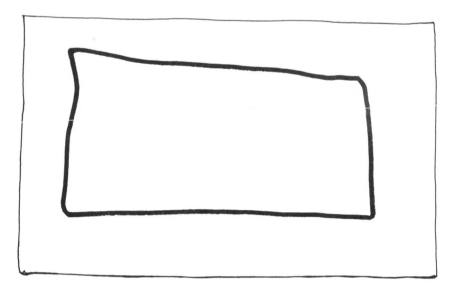

Although there are conflicting reports in the literature, it appears that the ability to draw figures arises from modifications of scribbling behavior rather than as reactions to external stimuli. Following this stage, the child will begin to draw irregular figures by combining curved and straight lines. A year later, he will be able to draw triangles and diamonds accurately.

First attempts to incorporate lateral lines into form drawing will usually be accompanied by rotating the paper. In essence, then, the child will still be drawing vertical and horizontal lines in constructing these figures. Later the child will be able to maintain a constant and straight orientation to the paper, keeping the paper parallel with the edge of the desk as he reproduces triangles and diamonds. Crosses incorporating lateral lines will also be used during these latter phases.

A recent study completed at our laboratory (and not published as yet) has produced findings which contribute to our understanding of the accuracy with which children of various ages draw basic geometric forms. One hundred seventy-nine children ranging in age from four to eight years were tested individually. While inspecting a circle, square, rectangle, triangle and diamond, the children were asked to draw an accurate copy of each figure.*

The four year olds could draw squares fairly accurately, but fifty per cent could not seem to close their circles. The four year olds were unable to draw rectangles, triangles or diamonds with any degree of accuracy.

By the age of five, the children were able to draw fair circles (closing them most of the time), squares, and rectangles, but still could not draw triangles or diamonds well.

*A detailed explanation of the scoring and administration of this test is found in the Appendix, p. 206.

The six year olds show a significant increase in their ability, when compared to the five year olds, to draw triangles and diamonds; and drew squares and circles equally as well as the five year olds.

The seven year olds were significantly better than the six year olds in the ability to draw squares, rectangles, triangles, and diamonds. The abilities of the eight year olds and the seven year olds did not differ significantly, thus suggesting that figure drawing ability in children tends to plateau about the age of seven.

Typical of the efforts of the children of various ages are the following:

	Circle	Square	Rectangle	Triangle	Diamond
Four Years					
Five Years					
Six Years					
Seven Years					
Eight Years					

Several other interesting findings emerged upon inspection of the data. Consistent from age to age and from figure to figure was the tendency of the more difficult figures to be drawn smaller than the easier ones. A size score was attached to each figure, and compilation of these indicated that given a figure to copy of the same size, rectangles were drawn smaller than squares, while the more difficult diamond was drawn smaller than the easier triangle. This tendency to restrict the size of the more difficult figures was slightly more pronounced in the older children.

Contrary to a common supposition, it was found that most children had more difficulty drawing an accurate circle than when asked to reproduce a square. At the same time, many of the children seemed to resist the simplicity of the drawing assignment given to them. They tried to draw faces in the circles and/or to make houses out of the triangles, and in other ways attempted to make the tasks more interesting. A detailed analysis of the *methods* used by the right-handed children in this investigation when drawing the various configurations is as follows.*

DRAWING CIRCLES. It was usual to find that a child began to draw a circle in the upper right hand portion, and usually proceeded clockwise at the age of five, with the tendency to draw counterclockwise more likely to be observed among the

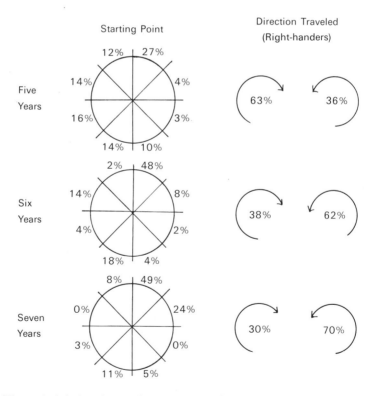

*The analysis is based upon the drawings of 46 five year olds, 50 six year olds, and 37 seven year olds, all right-handed children. The methods used by the left-handed children were not analyzed, as there were only 4, 7, and 5 subjects respectively in the three age groups.

six and seven-year-old right-handers. The graphs below portray the percentage of children of each age group beginning at various portions of the circle, and the percentage of children traveling in each direction.

DRAWING SQUARES, RECTANGLES, TRIANGLES, AND DIAMONDS. Three percentages were obtained upon tabulating the drawing methods of the children as they copied squares, rectangles, triangles, and diamonds; (a) the percentage starting at various portions in the figures, (b) the percentage who drew the figures continuously without lifting their pencils from the paper, and (c) the direction the children who drew continuously traveled with their pencils around the figures. The results are summarized below.

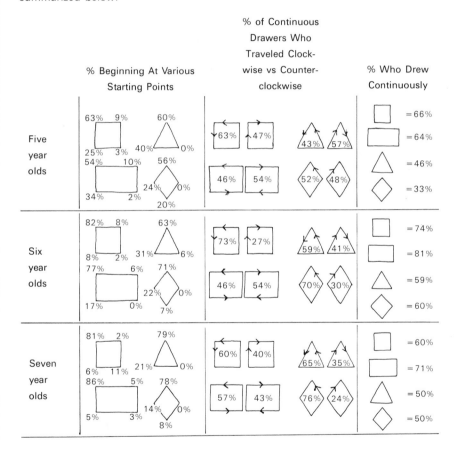

It is thus apparent upon inspection of these findings that, as might be expected, with increasing age children tend to draw these figures in a more continuous manner. In general, these right-handed children began their rectangles and squares in the upper left-hand corners. When drawing the more difficult triangles and diamonds, they began in the top corners and usually proceeded in a counterclockwise direction. Analysis of the directions the right-handed children of five years took when drawing all the figures reveals no clear-cut trends. They were as likely to move in a clockwise as in a counterclockwise direction. However, by the age of six and seven, most of right-handed children drew the figures by moving their pencils in a counterclockwise direction.

AGGREGATES AND COMBINES. Two overlapping phases in drawing behavior occur next. (*a*) Two forms will be placed in simple combinations to form patterns, and (*b*) these in turn will be incorporated into complex patterns, using three or more simple forms. Combines are combinations of two forms, while aggregates may be defined as combinations of more than two separate forms. Examples follow.

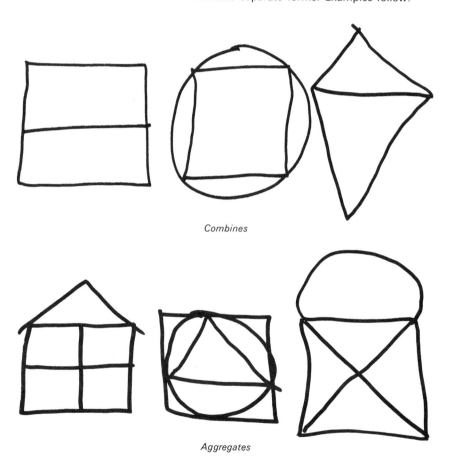

Combines

Aggregates

It has been hypothesized that the drawing of these latter types of figures by a child is influenced by teacher and parental stimulation. However, the intrinsic interest to the child for drawing such figures undoubtedly plays an important part in their practice.

A portion of the test developed for the assessment of graphic behavior of children measures the ability to reproduce an "aggregate" of a complex nature.

Recently this test has been given to 179 children, ages four to eight years, and the following results have emerged.* The task involves drawing one-by-one figures added to the corners of a square which the child first draws after observing the examiner draw it. The child is given an opportunity to see each new figure added to the total configuration so that the final pattern appears like this (reduced in size).

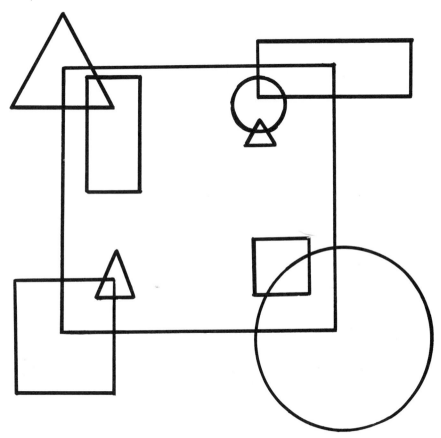

1. At the age of four, the children did not overlap any of the figures, pre-ferring to draw them separately. In addition, as would be expected, most of the figures appear as rounded squares or as ''squared-off'' circles. The inability to reproduce triangles and rectangles was apparent. Most of the four year olds could not locate any of the figures in proper relationship to each other (or perhaps did not feel it was important!).

2. By five the children were able to overlap one or two figures, and to locate 4 or 5 out of the 10 figures correctly. The triangles began to appear differently than the squares and circles at this age.

*Detailed test administration, scoring, and results are found in the Appendix, p. 205.

3. By six years of age, the children became able to locate most of the figures accurately (usually about 7 or 8 out of 10), and could draw the various figures reasonably well.

Typical of the Drawings in This
Task at Various Ages

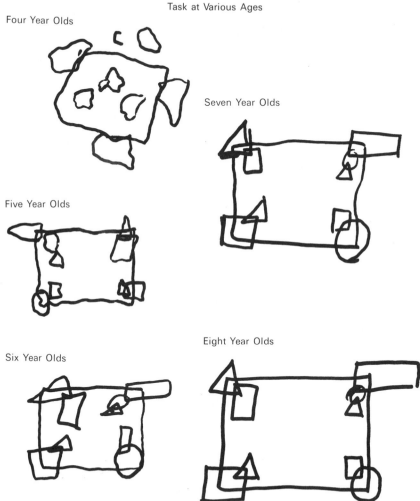

Four Year Olds

Seven Year Olds

Five Year Olds

Six Year Olds

Eight Year Olds

Pictorial Phase. The final stage in graphic behaviors has been termed the pictorial phase. Simple pictures which usually consist of familiar objects, houses, trees, the sun, and people are attempted by the child during this phase. I will restrict my discussion of the development of the graphic behavior in children to their motor development. The two areas I will exclude from the pictorial phase are: (a) the psychologist's use of human figure drawing to expose certain mental and emotional attributes which may lie dormant in children; (*b*) the artist's use of figure drawing to stimulate the creative potential of children.

The several stages through which the child passes in his attempts to draw human figures are:

a. Circles with marks in them or around them.

b. Circles with marks in and around them, assuming human form.

c. Circles with approximate representations of the parts of the face.

d. Round faces with legs and arms coming directly from the face.

e. The appearance of fingers and trunk.

or

f. The increased refinement of the figure, including emphasis on eyes, eyebrows, fingers, feet and attempts at facial expression.

By the age of five and six, then, the child deliberately draws parts of his environment, instead of producing them accidentally. Pictorial representations of depth and perspective appear in their drawings at about the age of eight and nine, while further refinements, including shading, appear later. These more advanced skills are highly related to any special training the child might have received during middle and late childhood.

Cursive Writing Versus Block Printing.   Between the seventh and eighth years, the child may be confronted with the problems of cursive writing, having earlier attempted to block print letters and numbers. A controversy exists concerning whether a child should first learn to print or to write cursively. Some arguments in favor of block printing are:

1. Block printing is not as difficult as cursive writing, nor does it require as much control.
2. If all cursive writing required the natural forward moving loops, it would be assumed to be the easier and more natural of the two. However, the frequent backtracking required when writing the letters a, s, o, p, for example, indicate that it is not as natural as some have suggested.

Arguments in favor of cursive writing include:

1. Cursive writing is more rhythmic than the disjointed block printing.
2. Letter reversal is not seen in cursive writing, while it is often found among five and six year olds attempting to print various asymmetrical letters and numbers.

After this very brief summary of the arguments favoring the two methods of teaching writing, a few general conclusions may help in determining which one to use. It would seem that some kind of modified block printing might be best for many children initially. It must be certain that movement patterns opposite to those later required for specific letters in cursive writing are not imposed on the child during this early block-printing training. Other children may profit from initial exposure to cursive writing, particularly those whose hand-eye control is reasonably well developed, and whose early attempts at spiral sequences seem relaxed and accurate.

Below are summarized sequences through which normal children usually pass in their attempts to acquire hand-eye control in drawing and writing movements.

REMEDIAL PROGRAMS

Two primary objectives are to be found in the various methods used to improve children's drawing and writing abilities. The aim of the first is to achieve more relaxation in writing movements. The second is to increase the control of writing movements.

It is believed desirable to combine tasks in programs of remediation which employ activities designed to enhance both accuracy and fluid movement. The

CHART 24

Drawing and Writing Movements

AGE (In years-months)	BEHAVIOR
15–18 months	Accidental and imitative scribbling.
1–1.6	Refinement of scribbles, vertical and horizontal lines, multiple line drawing, scribbling over visual stimuli.
2–3	Multiple loop drawing, spiral, crude circles. Simple diagrams evolve from scribblings by the end of the second year.
3	Figure reproduction to visually presented figures, circles, and crosses.
4	Laboriously reproduces squares, may attempt triangles but with little success.
4.6–5	Forms appear in combinations of two or more. Crude pictures appear (house, human form, sun). Can draw fair squares, crude rectangles, and good circles, but has difficulty with triangles and diamonds.
6–7	Ability to draw geometric figures matures. By seven can draw good circles, squares, rectangles, triangles, and fair diamonds.

teacher may alternate between the two types of tasks; if a child appears to be able to make relaxed coordinated movements in relatively large amounts of space, he should then require smaller more accurate movements. If attempting to make accurate movements required in block printing of letters and numbers appears to manifest itself in a tense, restricted manner, the educator should insert arm-freeing movement tasks into the program.

The overriding objective of programs designed to remediate hand-eye coordination in drawing tasks should be the development of a child who is flexible (*i.e.*, one who can write on a variety of writing surfaces in a number of planes, and one who can execute a number of types of movements in all directions relative to his body). The educator, then, should develop a program in which the child's nervous system is afforded a large variety of neuromotor "programs" so that his drawing-writing behavior will meet all academic and artistic contingencies with which he will be confronted.

Types of arm-hand-freeing exercises.

1. Repetitive circles, loops which "travel" . . .

2. Repetitive circles, figure 8's, in all planes which remain relatively fixed . . .

3. Repetitive lines in various planes, using large amounts of space . . . copied on blackboards, and/or on large sheets of paper . . .

We have not encountered any evidence that two-handed drawing tasks in which both arms move simultaneously, advocated by some authorities,[2] are productive of more efficient one-handed drawing accuracy. It would seem that practice time should be devoted primarily to one-handed movements with the child's preferred hand when executing the above exercises.

Hand preference may be assessed by noting the tendency of a child to use one hand or the other in 5 or 6 difficult (for him) one-handed tasks done during several testing periods lasting for two or three weeks. His preferred hand should be considered the hand most used in these tasks, even though the tendency to do so may be slight.

4. Drawing in many directions in several planes.

5. Drawing kinesthetically.

Types of accuracy-producing exercises.

1. Channel drawings

2. Dot-connecting

3. Template tracing

One of the more helpful methods of encouraging accurate hand-eye coordinations that are needed in drawing and writing has been outlined by Kephart, Strauss, and others.

    1. Initially, it is suggested that the hand be guided through various line and figure drawing tasks by the teacher. The child's hand should be held, and he should be encouraged to watch its movements as it is pulled through a number of desired configurations.

    2. Next it is suggested that the child be presented with apparatus which permit him to move a pencil or some other writing instrument down grooves shaped as circles, squares, and the like. Increased difficulty will be encountered when these figures are made smaller.

3. When the child is able to perform the exercises in #2 above (*i.e.* he does not ''jam'' the pencil in the groove, nor does he retrace his progress), he may be asked to draw various figures within shallow pans ot modeling clay (about ¼ inch deep). This exercise, while more difficult than drawing in channels, involves a media which to some degree ''grabs'' the writing instrument and prevents small inaccuracies in movement from becoming magnified.

4. After competency in drawing accurate figures in clay is developed, the teacher should present various patterns over which the child can trace. Various geometric figures, as well as line drawing of various shapes and in several directions, are included in this portion of the training program.

5. The final step requires that the child draw various patterns without tracing. Patterns are presented visually for the child to inspect and to copy. Then, the patterns should be visually presented for shorter periods of time before the child is permitted to start drawing, thereby enhancing his visual memory. A final stage would involve offering verbal directions concerning the type of line and/or geometric figure the teacher expects the child to draw.

In a recently completed study in our laboratory, the composite form drawings of 65 children described on page 85 were scored before and after participating in a program of motor education encompassing *primarily big muscle activities,* agility, balance, and the like. The mean time between the pre- and post-test was five months, and three scores were obtained reflecting whether the child copied the figures' sizes accurately, the accuracy with which they drew the figures, and whether they located the figures correctly as they added them to the diagram.

Analysis of the findings revealed that while no significant difference was obtained in the accuracy or size of the drawings when contrasting pre- and post-test scores, highly significant changes were obtained in the accuracy with which they *located* the figures on the various corners of the original square they drew to start the exercise. Out of a possible 10 points for locating each of the 10 figures correctly, the group of 65 with an average age of 8.92 (SD = 2.48), containing 58 boys and 7 girls, scored 5.29 (SD = 3.47) prior to participating in the program while the final score achieved on this type of complex drawing form drawing test was 7.04 (SD = 3.35), a difference significant at the 1 per cent level of confidence (t = 5.68).* It thus appeared that participation in activities involving total body movement may have contributed to the ability to organize figures in space when drawing on a page, although further research is needed before such a claim may be substantiated. A control group containing similar children is presently being tested in order to further validate this finding.

SUMMARY

A survey of the literature reveals several overlapping stages in the development of scribbling and drawing in children. By the age of five years, children begin to draw reasonably accurate squares and circles, but are unable to draw triangles and diamonds. By the age of seven, the ability to draw geometric figures and to locate them relative to each other tends to mature.

As a child matures, he tends to, if right-handed, draw geometric figures in a continuous manner in a counterclockwise direction. The more difficult figures are drawn smaller than simpler ones, other things being equal.

Remedial techniques for drawing should include tasks intending to improve accuracy, as well as those which encourage freedom of hand-arm movement. Accuracy may be improved by first guiding a child's hand, then asking him to draw through grooves; and if this can be accomplished, he may then draw in clay, later being asked to trace over figures, and finally to make free-hand figures of complexity. "Arm freeing" exercises should be engaged in, in various planes, and in various directions, relative to the child's body.

REFERENCES

1. Eberhard, Ulrich: "Transfer of Training Related to Finger Dexterity," *Percept. & Mot. Skills, 17,* 274, 1963.
2. Getman, G. N. and Kane, Elmer R.: *The Physiology of Readiness—An Action Program For the Development of Perception for Children,* Minneapolis, Minnesota, P.A.S.S. Inc., 1964.
3. Goodenough, F. L.: *Measurement of Intelligence by Drawings,* Yonkers, New York, World Book Co., 1926.
4. Illingworth, R. S.: *The Development of the Infant and Young Child—Normal and Abnormal,* 3rd Edition, Edinburgh, E. & S. Livingstone Ltd., 1967.

*The mean improvement which would be expected within a five-month interval according to normative data in our possession is .86 points; while the experimental group in this study evidenced a change of 1.75 points during this same time interval.

5. Kellogg, Rhoda: *What The Child Scribbles and Why,* Palo Alto, California, National Press, 1955.
6. Machover, Karen: *Personality Projection in the Drawing of the Human Figure (A Method Of Personality Investigation),* Springfield, Charles C Thomas, 1949.
7. Morris, Desmond: *The Biology of Art—A Study of the Picture-Making Behavior of the Great Apes and Its Relationship to Human Art,* New York, Alfred A. Knopf, 1962.
8. Swenson, C. H.: "Empirical Evaluations of Human Figure Drawings," *Psychol. Bull.; 54,* 431–466, 1954.
9. White, Burton L. and Held, Richard: "Plasticity of Sensorimotor Development in the Human Infant," *The Causes of Behavior: Readings In Child Development and Educational Psychology,* Judy F. Rosenblith and Wesley Allinsmith (ed.), Boston, Allyn Bacon, 1966.

7

Strength, Flexibility, and Endurance

It is a common finding that retarded children are muscularly unfit[5,7] (fitness usually implying some kind of efficiency encompassing performance in tasks which require muscular strength, flexibility, and/or cardiovascular endurance). The Joseph P. Kennedy, Jr. Foundation, in reacting to these findings, has instituted and financed programs of recreation and physical education in an effort to reverse this condition in retarded children.[1]

Retarded children face several situations which cause them to be physically unfit. The first involves the social rejection by normal peers experienced by retardates. Such rejection results in lessened opportunities to participate in vigorous games. Complex rules encountered in many sports and games may also exclude them from activities. The retardate is also faced with his own feelings of failure when neuromotor problems make him unfit for many activities. This lack of coordination results in a disinclination to participate, a situation which then results in decreased capacity to perform if vigorous muscular activity is not engaged in for long periods of time. Moreover, there is many times a lack of appropriate recreational facilities available to the retarded child.

Improving the fitness of retardates does not result solely through prescribing strict exercise regimens. A retardate told to do 10 or 20 pushups is not aware of the long-term "good" these exercises will do him for he is only concerned with the emotional content of his experiences (*i.e.,* are the exercises fun or oppressive). If they seem oppressive, it is unlikely that he will "overload" himself and perform the exercises with vigor. Unless these muscular exercises or endurance activities place an overload on the child, little or no change will occur.

When trying to improve the general fitness of retardates, one primary concern is the need to motivate them to participate vigorously. I believe that an increased tendency to participate in vigorous activities comes about when the child perceives he is becoming more competent in the skills required. Thus, skill improvement would seem to be a more productive way to better general and specific measures of muscular and respiratory fitness than an exercise program.

Acting on this principle, approximately five minutes at the end of an hour of physical activity is devoted specifically to fitness exercises in the program I administer at the University of California, Los Angeles.* A comparison of the scores of 15 children (mean age 9.3 years) in a pre- and post-test situation separated by five months of classes held twice a week was made. The following findings emerged: statistically significant improvement was obtained in the measures of pushing strength with the pre-test mean of 5.0 pushups (SD = 6.5), and a post-test mean of 9.6 pushups (SD = 4.8), (t = 3.28). Similar improvement was noted when comparing the pre- and post-test scores reflecting abdominal strength (sit-ups) and pulling strength (modified pullups). Mean score for sit-ups was 3.6, while the final mean was 6.4 (SD's 3.5 and 4.22 respectively, t = 2.78). Mean improvement in pullups was 3.4, with a pre-test average of 2.0, and a post-test average score of 5.4 obtained by the children.

During the first part of the hour, however, the children in this program performed a number of vigorous activities which undoubtedly contributed to the improvement shown. For example, ample time was allotted for trampoline jumping, an activity which requires rigid tension in the abdominal, stomach, and leg muscles as the child contacts the bed to achieve maximum height on successive bounces. The child will receive an uncomfortable whiplash type of reaction if he is limp when he contacts the bed of the trampoline.**

A survey of the literature suggests that the following principles be observed when exposing atypical children to exercise regimens:

1. The relatively high incidence of cardiovascular problems in populations of atypical children, particularly mongoloids, makes it advisable that each child be subjected to a reasonably thorough physical examination prior to the application of any vigorous program of exercises and endurance activities.

2. Passively performing exercises without any overload of the muscular and/or cardiovascular system will result in little or no improvement of endurance or strength. Exercises will extend the child's limits if he is encouraged to impose overloads on *himself.*

3. Strength exercises performed through a range of motion are probably superior to isometrics, particularly if improvement in limb strength is desired. Static exercises for developing trunk strength are sometimes desirable.

4. Endurance in muscular exercises can be improved if a circuit exercise program is used and several exercises are done in rapid succession with little rest between each exercise.

5. Muscular flexibility may be improved greatly by requiring the muscles to stretch for prolonged periods of time, rather than imposing the bouncing and stretching movements. Actually, the latter type of movement performed rapidly

---

*It is surprising how physical educators working with all children persist in administering vigorous exercises intended to overload the child's muscular systems at the *beginning* of the physical education period, instead of at the *end* of the period where such exercises more properly belong.

**Despite current hypotheses regarding the use of trampolines for helping some atypical children, I believe that the main benefits derived from trampoline jumping may be explained by improvement of trunk-leg fitness due to regular and vigorous demands made upon the anti-gravity muscles when bouncing.

may impede the acquisition of flexibility by damaging the tendinous muscle sheath, which tends to tighten up further the muscle tissue involved.

6. The exercise program should be designed to induce strength and flexibility in various areas of the body through the applications of specific exercises for specific body parts.

7. Exercise regimens to lose weight without accompanying diet control are usually ineffective. Most children and adults can defeat most programs of vigorous physical exercise by overeating.

8. Fat in specific spots of the body cannot be "worn off" by exercising muscles underlying this fat. Children will gain and lose fat in specific areas of the body as they generally lose and gain body weight. The amount of fat lost or gained in a specific body area is dependent upon the percentage of body fat characteristically carried by that individual in that area of his body.

STRENGTH

A complete catalogue of all possible strength exercises would encompass a manual many times the size of this one. A book by Wallis and Logan[9] contains detailed fitness exercises for children. Therefore, the following exercises are intended as suggested types of activities and ways in which they might be employed.

Four primary areas of the body will be dealt with, as well as exercises projecting various degrees of intensity and difficulty. Suggestions for exercising the shoulder-girdle, the abdominal region, the legs, and the lower back are listed below.

Arm-Shoulder Exercises. Pushing exercises aid the chest muscles, muscles in the front of the shoulder, and muscles which extend the arm. Examples of some appropriate exercises for children include:

Wall Pushups:

These may be made more difficult by moving the child back further from the wall, and/or requiring the hands to be placed further apart on the wall or closer than shoulder width.

Knee Pushups:

These also may be made more difficult when the hands are placed wider or narrower than shoulder width. When a child can do from 6 to 8, he should be encouraged to do:

Regular Pushups:

These are more difficult if the legs are raised about 1 foot as shown.

Pulling exercises are important for the upper back muscles. The "winged" scapulas frequently seen protruding from the backs of unfit children can be made to lie flat against the upper back if various pulling exercises are performed. For example:

Rope pulling, rising from a seat to a stand.

The child can "climb" and lower himself to a seated position again, using slow, controlled movements.

Horizontal pulling: hand-over-hand pulling can also be fun on a rope extending in horizontal directions; tug-of-war is a competitive pulling exercise.

If a child can perform the above exercises well, a modified pullup should be used. The feet should remain on the floor, and the body should remain straight as the pullup to a chest high bar is executed from 6 to 10 times.

Abdominal Lower Back. Abdominal exercises while lying on the back are more effective if the knees are slightly bent, causing the large leg muscles to be excluded from the movement.

Simple abdominal ''curls'' become harder if the flexed position is held for from four to eight seconds.

Full situps are helpful, and if the child twists from side-to-side, more trunk muscles are involved.

Situps can be made easier if the child reaches forward with his hands; it is more difficult to keep the hands behind the head when doing them.

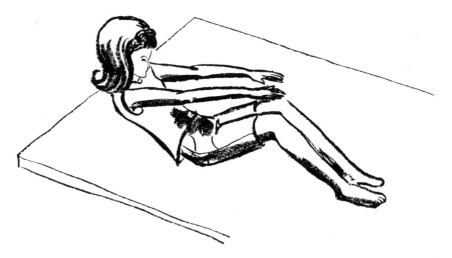

Lying on an incline, head down, of course, makes situps more difficult as does holding a weight behind the head. These latter two exercises are usually too difficult for most retarded children.

Simple back "extensions" are helpful when attempting to strengthen the lower back. If held from four to eight seconds, they become more effective. The ankles should be held down as shown, and the child should be encouraged to hold his arms in several different positions while performing them (i.e., behind his head, extended to the front, to the sides, etc.).

Back Extension.

Hands to the front in a back extension.

More difficult yet is when the child's upper body is permitted to drop below his hips while lying on a bench. Care must be taken to execute this modification slowly and should only be attempted when reasonable strength is evidenced in the simpler back extension movement described above.

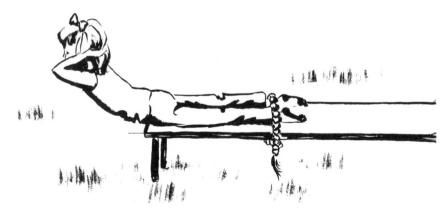

STRENGTH AND ENDURANCE

If strength exercises are performed within a short period of time, with little rest between each, cardiovascular endurance is enhanced. For example:

"Build-up" pushups (or any other exercise) can be accomplished by starting with one; jogging about 15 to 20 feet away and performing 2; jogging back to the original starting point and doing 3; and continuing until from 6 to 10 of the specific exercises are performed at one of the "stations."

This type of exercise regimen may have two or three stations in which various kinds of exercises are performed at each, and in which the number of exercises are increased or decreased as each station is reached, for example:

An exercise program of this nature may aid in the control of children who are emotionally disturbed, but physically competent. Care must be taken for extreme fatigue can result from its use due to the lack of recuperation time allowed between exercises. Higher motivation will result if exact daily records of improvement are kept for this and for other exercise programs outlined in these pages. Usually this type of vigorous exercise will not reduce the energies of hyperactive children. On the contrary, the children frequently become more difficult to control as the intensity of the exercise increases. Therefore, when following such a vigorous regimen with easily distracted children, a relaxation period should follow.

ENDURANCE

Activities solely intended to improve cardiovascular endurance may also be engaged in productively. Such as:

Alternate jogging and walking.

A distance of about 300 yards should be used to start with, jogging 50 and walking 50 yards; this can be gradually increased as the children become able to accommodate to the various overloads.

Swimming and activities to train competitive swimmers are used by some educators with success on neurologically impaired children.

Kicking for distance on kickboards; keep track of improvement.

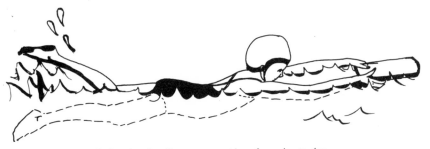

Swimming for distance; count laps from day to day.

Various running activities are helpful.

Distance in time; "How far can you go in five minutes?"

Time: "How long can you keep jogging?"

It is not to be expected that endurance gained by swimming will readily transfer to competency in running activities or vice-versa. These kinds of activities, however, since progress is so easily measured and perceived by the children participating, may have desirable "side-effects" related to improvement of the children's self-concept.

MUSCULAR FLEXIBILITY

Stretching should be done slowly and using the limb or trunk to their full range of movement.

Slow reaching for the toes while seated or standing is helpful in achieving flexibility in the lower back and back-of-the-leg muscles.[4] If this is done too vigorously, particularly with fast-growing children in late childhood or early adolescence, minor or major damage to the heel tendon may result.

Arm stretching exercises are helpful, simple equipment (towels) may be used.

Child should not pull outward with the towel, but should move his arms forward and backward stretching the shoulder.

Backward trunk flexibility as well as forward flexibility should be improved.

SUMMARY

Programs consisting solely of muscular exercises for children must be well motivated if they are to be beneficial. The duration of time devoted to them need not be prolonged, if the children are otherwise engaged in games and other developmental activities of a vigorous nature.

Records simple enough for the children to comprehend should be kept, so that progress may be observed by both participants and teachers. At times, several components of muscular and cardiovascular fitness may be improved at the same time as illustrated on page 108.

Fitness activities might be scheduled for from five to fifteen minutes, three times a week on a Monday-Wednesday-Friday basis, with the intervening days devoted to the improvement of manual dexterity and sports skills.

REFERENCES

1. AAHPER—Kennedy Foundation: Special Fitness Awards for the Mentally Retarded, Washington, D.C., NEA Publications.
2. Benda, Clemon, E.: *The Child With Mongolism,* New York, Grune & Stratton, 1960.
3. Cratty, Bryant J.: "Strength, Endurance Plus Flexibility Equals Fitness," Chapter VIII in *Developmental-Sequences of Perceptual-Motor Tasks,* Freeport, New York, Educational Activities, Inc., 1967.
4. DeVries, Herbert J.: Evaluation of Static Stretching Procedures for the Improvement of Flexibility, *Res. Quart.; 33,* 222–229, 1962.
5. Francis, R. J. and Rarick, G. L.: "Motor Characteristics of the Mentally Retarded," U.S. Office of Education Co-operative Research Project #152, University of Wisconsin, September, 1967.

6. Hayden, Frank J.: *Physical Fitness for the Mentally Retarded,* Washington, D.C., Joseph P. Kennedy Foundation, 1964.
7. Howe, Clifford: "A Comparison of Motor Skills of Mentally Retarded and Normal Children," *J. Except. Child.; 25*-8, 352–354, April, 1959.
8. Johnson, G., Orville: "A Study of the Social Position of Mentally Handicapped Children in the Regular Grades," *Am. J. Ment. Defic.; 55,* 60–89, 1950.
9. Wallis, E. and Logan G. A.: *Exercise for Children,* Englewood Cliffs, New Jersey, Prentice-Hall Inc., 1966.

8

Control of Large
Muscle Groups

It is difficult to separate the motor acts into two distinct categories such as those using large muscle groups and those involving small muscle groups because the majority of motor acts integrate muscles of both size. To cite an example, dribbling a basketball down the court incorporates fine muscular adjustments for the manipulative act of guiding the ball, and gross muscle action for the locomotor movements of running, pivoting, jumping, and leaping into the air. Moving from a sports oriented environment to an academic one, the large postural muscles are needed to stabilize the balance of the child while he is seated at his desk or standing at the blackboard, and his fine muscle movements are used in the manipulative skills of writing.

Fine integration and synchronization of muscle groups in the body is imperative to a child's efficient performance in some classroom tasks and on the playground. The synchronized movements of one side of the body with the other and of the arms with the legs are essential to the skills of jumping and throwing. The coordinated movements of the hand and eye are essential to mastering some academic skills. In Chapter 6, some activities were suggested to encourage motor control of the arm-eye action systems. This chapter will discuss types of activities to be used in developing balance as well as agility and ball-handling skills.

BALANCE

Balance is an essential factor for general motor performance. Frequently this attribute is evaluated under conditions where stress is placed on the individual so he is forced to orient his body in a difficult way to gravity. Good balance depends upon the interaction of two primary systems: the muscular feedback from the postural muscles which control the ability to maintain an upright position, and the visual system which aids the individual to "tie-himself-down" to gravity when a variable has been imposed on him to create disequilibrium.

Several research studies have discovered that retarded children as a group do not balance as well as do normal children. For example, Howe[1] found among the group of retardates he surveyed the mean time for balancing on one foot to be no more than fifteen seconds as contrasted with scores obtained from a population of normal children whose mean time for balancing on one foot was fifty-three seconds. A correlation of $+.45$ was obtained from data recently compiled in a study conducted in the perceptual-motor learning laboratory at the University of California when balance scores were contrasted with scores from the Gates Reading Survey. Supportive evidence is found in a study by Ismail who obtained similar low to moderate correlations between the same two measures of balance and reading.[3]

It would thus appear that the visual-motor coordination underlying balance is to a slight degree predictive of reading success. A correlation of .4, however, only means that about 16 per cent of the manner in which children's reading scores arranged themselves (from best to worst) is predictable from knowing their balance scores.

After evaluating the results of these studies, there seems to be no indication that improved balance will influence a variety of perceptual attributes. However, improvement in balance is important for its own sake because of its effect upon other motor attributes.

It is possible to improve balance in children through specially designed programs and over a comparatively short period of time. Of the 51 children who participated in a motor training program at University of California, Los Angeles, which extended over a period of five months, 71 per cent of the children manifested a significant improvement. The pre- and post-testing scores demonstrated a change approximating one year on a muturation scale.

Several general considerations should be kept in mind when attempting to train a child to balance better.

1. Training should take place in several kinds of balance tasks including those in which some kind of visual stress is imposed, (*i.e.,* eyes-closed balance tasks), in tasks in which the child is asked to move and maintain his equilibrium (beam walking), as well as in activities in which his center of mass remains relatively fixed (static balances of various sorts).

2. Balancing may be made increasingly difficult for a child by imposing stresses of several kinds.

   a. The area on which the child is balancing may be made smaller (decrease the width of the balance beam).

   b. Some kinds of visual stress may be imposed, ranging from the easiest (watch a stable point), through increasingly difficult, (specific instructions about what should be done with the eyes) to requiring the child watch a moving point which moves from left to right across the line or beam the child is attempting to walk.

   c. The platform on which the child is asked to balance may be made increasingly unstable. An example is asking him to balance on a small board with some kind of runner or knob underneath it.

   d. In static balances, the child's base of support may be decreased or his center or mass may be raised . . . *i.e.,* stand on one foot . . . lift your arms (or knee) higher.

Although the outline presents the activities in sequence, in actually working with children, the balance tasks should be both static and dynamic in nature, and the tasks used should become progressively more difficult.

When asking a child to assume the positions suggested in the illustrations, he should be given the position he finds reasonably difficult to maintain. Encourage him to maintain the position for four to eight seconds; then increase the time interval from eight to ten seconds in the more difficult positions using some of the techniques suggested in the outline which follows.

These static balance positions may be assumed on the trampoline for additional difficulty.

1. *Static Balance.*   Static balance tasks may involve posturing in standing positions of various kinds, and/or balancing in relatively stable positions on mats, with the arms, knees, elbows, head, etc., touching the mat. Generally, these activities should be made interesting to children by using various kinds of imagery. For example, it may be suggested that they make "bridges" with themselves over the "river" (lines drawn on the floor).

For example:

Low bridges, using various parts of the body in contact with the mat. Knees, hands, elbows, etc.

Higher bridges, using hands, feet, and combinations of each.

Bridges with the back toward the mat.

These games can, of course, be made into left-right training games, as the child is asked to remove certain arms and legs from the mat, or the balance on his left-foot and right-arm, etc. Later, the child can be asked to create various types of bridges, *i.e.,* use three parts of your body, one of which is an elbow; use two parts of your body, one of which is a knee.

Various standing positions can be employed, with modifications of arms and leg positions which can be made increasingly difficult.

Line standing positions, both feet on lines in various ways . . . arms on shoulders, folded, and overhead . . . for added difficulty.

One foot stand positions, using preferred and non-preferred foot, with arms involved in the balance, folded in front of the body, on shoulders, over head.

Both "bridges" games and standing balances can be made easier if the child is asked to watch a point while balancing as shown.

At the same time, both types of static balancing activities can be made more difficult by asking the child to assume various of the positions with the eyes closed.

Additional difficulty can be introduced if the standing positions are assumed, while asking the child to watch a moving point, *i.e.,* a ball swinging on a string.

Balance Platforms. The balance quality probably needed when skating, skateboarding, surfing and the like can be aided by using platforms that move on one or two axes as shown below.

By modifying the positions the child stands, increasing difficulty can be introduced. Also, by either asking the child to fixate at a given point, or to close his eyes, or to watch moving points, *i.e.*, play catch with another child on a similar balancing platform, increased difficulty can be introduced.

Modifications of foot positions

Arm positions can be also modified

One-footed balances can be assumed

When a child is asked to assume the positions outlined in the previous illustrations, he should be given positions which he finds reasonably difficult to maintain, those which he can hold for from four to eight seconds. After he can maintain various positions for about eight to ten seconds, more difficult positions, visual stresses, balancing methods should be introduced.

MOVING BALANCES

You can vary the nature of the platform walked by raising it from lines on the floor to beams of various heights.

Narrow it . . .

Tilt it to the left or right . . .

Incline it for up-hill or down-hill walking . . .

Several children may be asked to perform various static balances at the same time using the width of the balance beam . . .

Other modifications of the surface may be made; objects may be placed on it to walk over . . .

Obstacles may be placed slightly above the surface of the beam . . .

Obstacles may be placed so that the child must walk under them . . .

You may ask the child to watch stable and later moving points as he becomes able to walk the beam with little effort.

Fixed points at the end of the beam . . . level with the eyes . . .

Fixed points to the side of the beam . . .

Moving points at the end of the beam moving up and down . . .

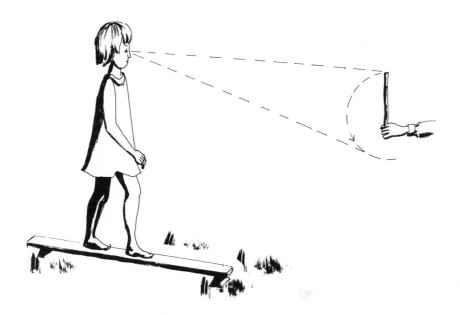

Moving points at the end of the beam, moving from side-to-side . . .

Moving points at the side of the beam, moving from side-to-side . . .

AGILITY MOVEMENTS

Agility movements of several kinds should be practiced by children, including those in which arm-leg integration is involved, those in which the body-movement is primarily up and down, and tasks which require that the body move forward-backward and from side-to-side in various rolling and locomotor activities.

Examples of some of these activities follow.

Arm-Leg Integration
Modified jumping jacks, in standing positions . . .

Both arms moving, with legs together and jumping . . .

Arm and leg on one side, apart and close to the body . . .

Both arms and legs apart and together at the same time . . .

Practice of this kind can be aided if the child is permitted to watch himself in a mirror.

Using a trampoline gives the child additional time to integrate arm-leg move-ments, but imposes additional anxiety, and the need for good stability as the bed of the trampoline is contacted.

Arm-leg interactions may be done in a horizontal plane, in a back-lying position. Both arms, moving at once, arms and legs on the same side, arms and legs moving together.

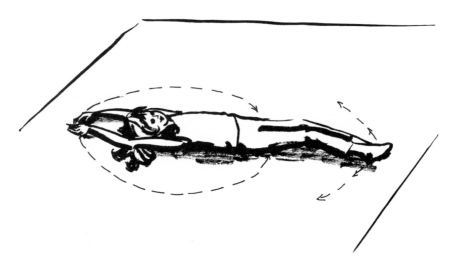

Additional complexity can be gained by asking these movements in the mat to be performed either slowly or rapidly.

Up-Down Activities In a Fixed Position
Getting up and down may be done in various ways . . . to the back, front, side, slowly, and rapidly . . . in various combinations.

Turn and get down, up, etc., can be done in various combinations and in reaction to various left-right directions.

Jumping up and turning to the left or right can be accomplished in various ways, specific jumping practice should be engaged in, helping the child to lift his arms as his legs extend.

Increased difficulty can be imposed if the jumps and turns are made over low obstacles, or the landings are on the same or different foot than the take-off.

Children should be taught to land properly when jumping from various heights.

Traveling Agility
Axis of the body near the mat and horizontal.

Various rolling movements can be accomplished.

Log rolling in various combinations.

From all fours to all fours.

Rolling in a ball, clasping the knees, using various axes of the body.

Rolling down-hill, individually.

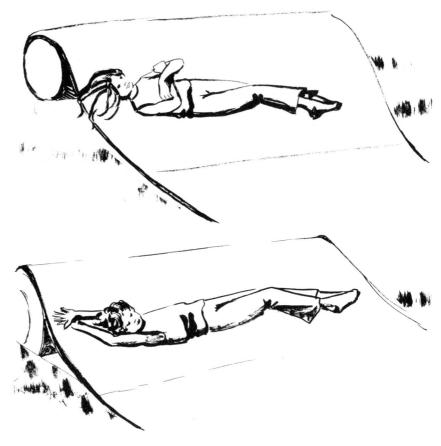

Or in pairs.

Locomotor Agility. A variety of agility tasks involving various locomotor skills may be incorporated into the child's program.

Crawling, requiring the child to place his hands into handprints.

Walking, requiring placement of feet into footprints.

Jumping forward over lines . . . and sideways.

Hopping forward, and sideways.

Jumping backwards.

Hopping backwards.

Skipping and galloping.

BALL HANDLING SKILLS

Throwing.   Simple lead-up drills, using only arm movements, and leg-body shift separately might precede throwing movements using both arm and leg movements . . . later practice may be obtained using a ball.

Arm movements only.

Leg-weight shift only.

A tipping platform may be used.

Arm and leg-weight shift without ball.

Arm-leg-weight shift with ball.

Increased accuracy in placement of ball on vertical and horizontally placed targets.

Vertical

Horizontally placed targets.

Ball Catching. Again lead-up activities should be used. Ball catching becomes harder, of course, when the ball is thrown faster, the ball used is smaller or when its pathway through space is unpredictable* from one trial to the next.

Ball rolling.

Watching, touching, and later attempting to catch balls swinging on strings.

Left-to-right.   Near-to-far.

In circles around the child.

In circles in front of the child.

In various planes with the child in a back-lying position.

Left-to-right in a back lying position is more difficult than:

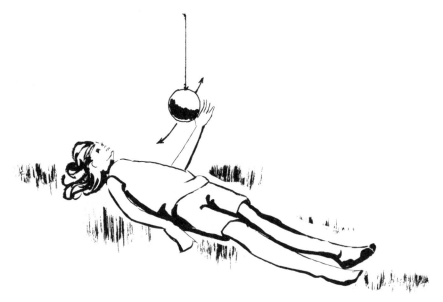

From head-to-foot.

Ball may be bounced . . . first larger ones.

And later thrown from a wide variety of angles.

Batting Balls.   A sequence of activities leading toward striking a ball with a bat has been found to be helpful when attempting to improve the skill of inept children within our program at the University of California at Los Angeles. Initially, the child may be asked to hit with a bat a rolled or fixed volleyball on the ground in front of him.

Next he may be asked to hit a volleyball fixed on a batting "T."

The volleyball may be bounced to him for additional difficulty.

Finally, the volleyball may be thrown to him, followed by trials in which balls of decreasing size are used, if he is successful in hitting the larger one.

In a recently completed unpublished study carried out in our laboratory, 15 retarded children (EMRs) were tested before and after participating for five months in a clinic program in which they engaged in activities intended to improve their assessed ineptitudes for a period of one hour, twice a week (either Monday-Wednesday or Tuesday-Thursday). The mean age of the group was 8.80 years (SD = 1.90). Thirteen were boys, while two were girls. The test battery used has been employed in other studies by the author, and is described on page 204 of the Appendix.

The improvement in the mean score for the battery was highly significant (1 per cent level). The pre-test mean was 32.13 (SD = 12.68), while the post-test average was 37.66 (SD = 10.65) (t = 3.74). During a five-month period, a group of normal children this age could be expected to improve only about 1.63 points in the mean score for the battery of six tests, while the retardates subjected to the program described improved several times this much or 5.53 points. The most improvement was evidenced in the sub-tests evaluating catching balls, gross agility, and locomotor agility.

SUMMARY

The improvement of control of the larger muscles in the body should include tasks intended to improve balance, agility, ball-handling skills and the like. Such tasks should be presented in a carefully planned sequential manner, from the simple to the more difficult, as the child's ability dictates.

Research indicates that a program containing the activities described in this chapter will elicit a significant improvement in the basic motor attributes of children. Special efforts should be made to include a variety of balance activities, encouraging the improvement of both static and moving balance, locomotor agility, as well as general bodily agility and ball-throwing as well as ball-catching skills.

The activities contained in this chapter should be modified as the instructor assesses the individual needs of his students.

REFERENCES

1. Howe, Clifford, "A Comparison of Motor Skills of Mentally Retarded and Normal Children, *J. Except. Child.* April 1959, 25, 8, 352–354.
2. Cratty, Bryant J.: *Developmental Sequences of Perceptual-Motor Tasks-Movement Activities For Neurologically Handicapped And Retarded Children and Youth,* Freeport, L.I., Educational Activities, Inc., 1967.
3. Ismail, A. H. and Gruber, J. J.: *Motor Aptitude and Intellectual Performance,* Columbus, Ohio, Charles E. Merrill, 1968.

9

Music and Rhythm

To an increasing degree, music and various rhythmic activities are becoming popular in educational programs for atypical children. In one program of perceptual-motor training, for example, all movements are executed to a beat. Further, music therapy has become a common part of programs in educating the retarded and emotionally disturbed.

Music is utilized in two primary ways: (a) The children are directed to respond to and conform to various musical beats. Sound and/or visual stimuli are used to accomplish this. (b) Music provides a rhythmic background for various types of perceptual-training regimens.

The research outlining the influence of music and rhythmic activity can be grouped into several categories. The first category concerns the effect music therapy has upon retarded children and adults. A second category investigates the manner in which rhythmic accompaniment aids the development of motor skills by normal children. Further, one interesting line of research reveals possible links between rhythmic ability and certain academic skills.[19, 20]

Many of the earlier studies claiming to outline the benefits of music therapy were more anecdotal than scientific in nature.[14, 22, 13, 8] In general, these studies reported findings which indicated that retarded and emotionally disturbed children became more outgoing, more aware of their surrounding environment, and more proficient in speech and motor skills after the incorporation of music into their research programs. The greatest success in such programs are recorded when severely retarded children are exposed to stimulating rhythmics involving a variety of sensory input, including flag displays, sounds, and the children's own movements.[18]

More recent investigations, however, have confirmed the worth of music as therapy in more scientific ways. Fitzpatrick,[5] for example, found that the severely retarded improved in tasks of manual dexterity when music was coupled with a voice familiar to his adult subjects. Harrison and others[10] found that music, when combined with exercises, exerted a significant positive effect upon various manual skills including buttoning buttons of different sizes, and the severely retarded's reactions to verbal commands (*i.e.,* "sit down," "pick up a ball," etc.). Harrison's program lasted twenty minutes a day, five days a week for a period of four weeks. In both studies cited, an attempt was made to obtain exact performance measures and control groups were used.

Other researchers have found that teaching motor activities of a rhythmic nature (*i.e.,* swimming, playing musical instruments) may exert a significant positive effect upon performance and learning.[4] There is research, however, which indicates that the ability to imitate a pattern of rhythm is not necessarily indicative of high skill levels in a variety of big muscle activities.

Researchers have also attempted to link rhythmic ability and reading. Sterritt and Rudnick completed two studies which indicate that rhythmic ability influences first and second graders' early attempts to read. These researchers report that by the third grade, factors other than the ability to fragment time into rhythmic patterns begin to influence reading ability.[19, 20] Such studies, however, merely suggest relationships; they do not prove that training in rhythmic tasks will cause reading to improve. Further research is needed to provide evidence that rhythmic training of various kinds aids speech, writing, and reading, all of which may require rhythm.

The "natural" preferences a child evidences in tasks such as tapping speed and walking speed are important influences upon his ability to copy rhythmic patterns. Research by Rimoldi[17] and others,[9] reviewed by Cratty,[3] indicates that certain "personal tempos" are relatively consistent from time to time, within specific parts of the body, and yet we cannot predict an individual's personal tempo in one part of his body (*i.e.,* hand tapping) by knowing how fast he prefers to move another part (*i.e.,* foot tapping). For example, it is not valid to say that an individual is "naturally slow moving" in a general way since it is usually not possible to predict the walking speed of an individual by known his preferred speed in leg tapping. At the same time, however, prefered tempos within specific parts of the body are consistent over time. The speed with which an individual arises from a seated position, for example, remains constant over a reasonably long period of time.[3]

Thus, when we ask a child to duplicate a rhythmic pattern, his ability and inclination to do so are probably influenced to some degree by the speed he *prefers* to move when no stimuli are present. Consequently, some children will resist moving rapidly in a given task, despite the characteristics of the music and "beat" they are to duplicate, while others will move too rapidly, despite their exposure to a slow tempo.

Some emotionally disturbed, blind, and retarded children display rocking movements of the head and body, rhythmic slapping, and other similar behaviors. Although the genesis of these movements are not understood well, several reasons have been posited to account for these "blindisms." Included is the suggestion that these inappropriate behaviors are a method of self-stimulation and heighten the child's awareness of his body. Such rhythmic movements, however, may interfere with the child's ability to learn, to relate to more appropriate stimuli, and to interact socially with his well-adjusted peers and parents. Therefore, while in some children it may be advisable to *establish* rhythmic movement patterns, others would profit from an *elimination* or *dimunition* of extraneous rhythmic activity.

To summarize, various types of rhythmic activities and background music may aid:

1. the acquisition of rhythmic motor skills among normal children;
2. the alertness of some retarded children;
3. retarded children to engage in perceptual-motor skills;
4. the initial learning of speech, reading, and writing.

For those interested in experimenting with using music as a form of therapy, certain basic ideas may prove helpful. Rhythmic stimuli (music, visual demonstration, etc.) have varying effects upon children, serving to excite some, while calming others. Moreover, rhythmic activities may, due to lack of concordance with a preferred tempo, be difficult for some children. Therefore, special care should be taken to present rhythmic activities in progressions to children with learning problems by varying the nature and speed of the stimuli. The complexity of the child's expected reaction should be considered in finding reasonable methods conducive to effective learning.

Several important considerations should be kept in mind when devising rhythmic activities for children with learning difficulties. The intensity of the stimuli should be kept within optimum limits; a noise too loud or too soft will not have the desired effect. The complexity of the stimuli should be arranged in order of increasing difficulty; attempting to react to an uneven beat is more difficult than reacting to a beat separated by even time intervals. Some rhythmic responses may be too complex for a child since he must use other components of the body to perform the task. Possibly this last point needs to be explained more fully.

The execution of rhythmic patterns in which more than one part of the body is involved are more complicated than the execution of a tempo in which only one limb moves. For example, hopping alternately on one foot and then on the other involves the use of balance, agility, comprehension, and neuromuscular skills to transform the directions into movement patterns. However, rhythmic movements involving just the use of the hands do not involve balance or other complex postural adjustments the hopping pattern requires. Perhaps the most difficult movement patterns are to be found in some of today's dancing patterns in which different tempos are being responded to simultaneously in several parts of the body.

Rhythm is the basis of many of life's movements and is observable in many acts performed by man. Yet little data are available in which rhythmic movements and music have been used in perceptual-motor research programs. The few suggestions to be found in this chapter are merely recommendations; they need to be explored in further research.

SEQUENCES

Body-Part Involvement. Rhythmic patterns may be translated into movements of various body parts as the child seats himself.

Rhythmic arm movement using the preferred arm with the other arm and legs immobile is probably the easiest to execute.

Rhythmic movement of only the preferred leg in response to a steady beat in a moderate tempo is slightly more difficult.

Alternating movement of the arms in response to a steady tempo is next in order of difficulty.

Alternating leg movement while seated is more difficult.

Movement that incorporates alternate arm-leg action on one side, followed by simultaneous arm-leg movements on the other side of the body is more complex.

A further progression in complexity is a movement that involves first one arm, then the other arm, and one leg, then the other leg until all four limbs are moved one at a time. Essentially, the movement "travels" from arm to arm, and then from leg to leg, and back again.

The movement of greatest difficulty is one which "travels" diagonally from arm to opposite leg, then to the second arm, and finally to the second leg.

Alternate Hopping Movements.   Alternate hopping patterns are difficult for most normal children five to eight years old to execute, as explained in Chapter 5, page 60. To expect retarded children, many of whom have motor problems, then, to perform different hopping movements which "travel" from leg to leg is unrealistic.

Rhythmic walking and skipping movements are heightened by introducing hopping patterns in stages. The child should first master stationary hopping patterns while seated. After this has been accomplished, the child may increase his proficiency by supporting himself with his hand on the back of a chair. When he has mastered sufficient stability, the child may be asked to hop or skip without support of any kind.

Research has indicated that the following temporal patterns represent a reasonable order of difficulty for this kind of task.[12]

It is easiest to hop alternately three times on one foot and then three times on the other. In a recent study, it was found that about 60 per cent of a group of eight-year-old boys were able to accomplish this movement pattern.[12]

A pattern slightly more difficult to execute consists of two hops on one foot and then two on the other. Only about 50 per cent of the eight-year-old boys could accomplish this without hesitation, while only about 35 per cent of the seven-year-old boys could execute this pattern.[12]

A very difficult kind of rhythmic hopping task (and probably most difficult when alternate arm movements are used) is one in which one foot executes an uneven number of hops, while the other foot executes an even number. A three-two tempo, for example, was found to be accomplished by 30 per cent of a group of eight-year-old boys, while 10 per cent of a group of seven-year-old boys could copy a demonstration of this kind of movement without touching both feet to the ground at the same time.[12]

Complexity of Stimuli.   Research by Bérges and Lézine[2] concerning the imitation of gesture, as well as other studies lend insight into the manner in which the nature and the complexity of the stimuli influence a child's ability to duplicate a pattern in movement.

Easiest to perform is probably reactions to even tempos when both visual and auditory stimuli are presented simultaneously. The vivid flag waving indigenous to the splendid program outlined by Robins,[18] for example, may elicit the attention of a severely retarded child who is out of contact with his environment much of the time. The rippling sound of the flags as they moved rapidly in front of the child, their bright colors,and movements of the flags may attract his attention. Thus, the child may begin, slowly at first, to react to this activity because these intense stimuli enter his consciousness through several channels at the same time.

Some children react better to visual than to auditory stimuli. In reacting to visual stimuli, it is easier for a child to respond to a single movement of a demonstrator than to any simultaneously presented rhythmic movement using more than one limb and without any auditory cues.

Auditory cues are often supportive of visual demonstrations, and they facilitate learning for the child. The well-conceived program evolved by Carl Orff[16] is one of several in which a "rhythm band" is used by retardates to produce music.[11]

After visual demonstrations of movement using only one body part, to increase the complexity of the act, the visual demonstrations may be presented to the children in which the demonstrator moves various body parts simultaneously.

To further increase the complexity of the activity, auditory cues are presented in an even tempo to accompany the child's movements.

SUMMARY

The following general guidelines should be followed in constructing a program of rhythmics for retarded children.

1. Reasonable sequences should be used in which responses and/or stimuli are placed in order of difficulty.

2. Since music and rhythm may either excite or calm a child, the teacher should attempt to bring the child's arousal level closer to the average through carefully controlling the tempo and intensity of the stimuli (Distractible children should be exposed to less intense stimuli and to slower beats; lethargic children should be exposed to tempos and stimuli which will raise their level of excitation. This heightened excitation is needed before the latter can be helped to learn better).

3. As children attend in unpredictable ways to various types of stimuli, visual *and* auditory stimuli either alone or in combination, should be used when working with children who are difficult to "reach."

4. Different speeds should be employed in presenting stimuli at beats comparable to a child's personal tempo to "break" a child "out" of habitual movement speeds. Flexibility of rhythm should be a goal.

REFERENCES

1. Alvin, J.: "The Response of Severely Retarded Children To Music," *Am. J. Ment. Defic.; 63,* 988–996, 1959.
2. Berges, J. and Lezine, L.: *The Imitation of Gestures,* Spastics Society Medical Education and Information Unit Association, London, William Heinemann, Medical Books, Ltd., 1965.
3. Cratty, Bryant J.: "Personal Equations in Movement," Chapter 12, *Movement Behavior and Motor Learning,* 2nd Ed., Philadelphia, Lea & Febiger, 197–207, 1967.
4. Dillon, Evelyn K.: "A Study of The Use of Music As an Aid In Teaching Swimming," *Res. Quart.; 23,* 1–8, 1952.
5. Fitzpatrick, F. K.: "The Use of Rhythm in Training Severely Subnormal Patients," *Am. J. Ment. Defic.; 63,* 981–987, 1959.
6. Fraser, L. W.: "Music Therapy For the Retarded Child," *Music Therapy,; 6,* 55, 1955.
7. Goldsmith, Carolyn; "The Use of Rhythmic Patterning For Neurologically Handicapped Children," Reprint 102 from *Academic Therapy Quarterly;* 1–2, DeWitt Reading Clinic, San Rafael, California.
8. Harbert, W. K.: "Some Results From Specific Techniques in the Use of Music With Exceptional Children," *Music Therapy; 2,* 133, 1955.
9. Harrison, R. and Dorcus, R.: "Is Rate of Voluntary Bodily Movements Unitary?," *J. Gen. Psychol.; 18,* 31–39, 1938.
10. Harrison, Wade, Lecrone, J., Temerlin, M. K., and Rousdale, W.: "The Effect of Music and Exercise Upon the Self-Help Skills of Non-Verbal Retardates," *Am. J. Ment. Defic.; 279–282, 71,* 1966.
11. Keller, Wilhelm: "Lecture on Orff-Schulwerk Around the World," Delivered at the First International Symposium on Orff-Schulwerk in the United States, May 2, 1967. (Bellflower City Schools, California).

12. Keogh, Jack F. and Pedigo, P.: "An Evaluation of Performance on Rhythmic Hopping Patterns," Sponsored by National Institute of Child Health and Human Development, UCLA, (Unpublished).

13. Loven, M. S.: "Value of Music Therapy for Retarded Children," *Music Therapy; 6,* 165–171, 1956.

14. Murphy, M. M.: "A Large Scale Music Therapy Program for Institutionalized Low Grade and Middle Grade Defectives," *Am. J. Ment. Defic.; 63,* 268–273, 1958.

15. Nordoff, P. and Robbins, Cline: *"Music therapy for Handicapped Children: Investigations and Experiences,"* New York, Music Publishers Holding Corporation.

16. Orff-Schulwerk: Basic Musical Forms for Orff-Schulwerk Classes in the Elementary School, Mineo. Bellflower School District, Bellflower, California.

17. Rimoldi, H. J. A.: "Personal Tempo," *J. Abn. & Soc. Psychol. 46,* 283–303, 1951.

18. Robins, Ferris, and Robins, Jennet: *Educational Rhythms for Mentally Handicapped Children,* New York, Horizon Press, 1965.

19. Rudnick, Mark, Sterritt, Graham M. and Flax, Morton: "Auditory and Visual Rhythm Perception and Reading Ability," *Child Devel.; 38-*2, 581–587, June, 1967.

20. Sterritt, Graham M. and Rudnick, Mark: "Auditory and Visual Rhythm Perception in Relation to Reading Ability in Fourth Grade Boys," *Percept. & Mot. Skills; 22,* 859–864, 1966.

21. ———: "Reply to Birch and Belmont," *Percept. & Mot. Skills; 23,* 632, 1966.

22. Weigl, V.: "Functional Music: Therapeutic Tool in Working With the Mentally Retarded," *Am. J. Ment. Defic.; 63,* 672–678, 1959.

10

Self-Confidence,
the Body-Image,
and Game Preferences

A child's total self-concept is a collection of feelings about many things. One very important component of his self-concept is the child's feelings about his own capacity to perform motor tasks. Basic to physical performance is his "vehicle" for movement, his body.

It is common to find among populations of atypical children an inordinate number of boys. For the male child in particular, proficiency in sports and his physique represent important variables which determine his self-confidence or feelings of inferiority.

The female, particularly in late childhood and early adolescence, usually has definite feelings about the conformations of her body. Her developing figure and the extent to which it resembles acceptable norms of the adolescent girl are of vital importance to her. It would seem, then, that the bodies of both normal or atypical males and females and their performance capacities and physical characteristics represent important components of their total self-concept.

In this chapter, several facets of a child's self-concept will be explored. Literature on the subject is reviewed and operational practices are recommended which pertain to body-image, components of the self-concept related to physical performance and appearance, aspiration level, and children's perceptions of games they enjoy playing. Game choice, stated opinions of performance potential, as well as measurable aspects of the body-image are inter-related in obvious and subtle ways. Some of these relationships are also explored, while the elucidation of others await further research.

THE SELF-CONCEPT OF RETARDATES

The data from recent studies indicate that retarded children whose mental capacities permit reasonably accurate self assessments of their intellectual and/or physical ineptitude suffer from feelings of inferiority.[4,6] These feelings may mani-

161

fest themselves in several ways and include withdrawal from activities, refusal to begin new activities, and other more pronounced emotional and behavioral disturbances. To counteract these symptoms, it is usually suggested that retarded children be placed in situations where they can achieve some success even though moderate.

Evaluation of the self-concept of retarded children is difficult. Their answers to direct questions may be invalid since their vocabulary is limited and they may misinterpret some questions. Their responses to various projective tests of personality assessment are similarly unpredictable and are likely to reflect something that just happened in the classroom that day rather than being a reflection of any deep attitude. The results of projective tests are also difficult to interpret since the results of drawing freely or finger painting, which are used to reflect personality traits in a child's self-concept, are affected by the inadequate perceptual-motor functioning in populations of retardates.

The use of self-report methods of assessment as well as projective techniques requires a third grade level of reading comprehension which many young retardates do not possess. I have used a self-report test, though, in the assessment of educable retardates (I.Q.'s about 70) with some success. For children whose abilities fall below this level, however, some kind of observational measure would be advisable.

Gallagher[9] has proposed a tentative solution to the evaluation of the self-concept of the lower-level retardate by using a rating scale to categorize atypical children according to their general level of personality development. These levels include:

Isolation: The child pays little attention to other people, does not seek affection, and does not try to communicate with other children or adults.

Dependency: The child has low opinion of his own skills, reacts to new problems by clinging to adult figure, does little unless told by an adult, and is totally defeated if rebuffed by adult upon whom he is dependent.

Omnipotence: The child displays an unjustified high opinion of himself, tries to bully and control others around him, and throws tantrums when interfered with.

Adult Imitation: The child prefers company of adults rather than those of his same age, and follows adults around seeking their affection.

Adult Identification: The child attaches himself to one specific adult, copies his values and behavior, and worships him as a hero.

Peer Imitation: The child prefers the company only of peers, follows peers around seeking their acceptance.

Peer Identification: The child attaches himself to one specific peer, copies his values, and worships him as a hero.

Self Determination: The child thinks for himself, and will oppose others if his own values dictate such opposition, realizes his limitations and works within them.

It is probable that a retardate will evidence behavior within a single day which corresponds to several of these levels. When rating children, it is necessary to select the level most frequently evidenced and to use two or more observers so that inter-observer reliability may be ascertained. It, however, may not be desirable for a low-level retardate to pass on to the self-determination level because his limitations may be so great that imitation of responsible peer or of adult behaviors is more desirable than independence. In any case, it is believed that this rating scale is a helpful one when attempting to evaluate the general self-concept and personality development of retardates possessing poor verbal comprehension.

THE BODY-IMAGE

Within recent years the body-image concept has appeared in literature encompassing a number of disciplines. To some writers, it is a key through which the total self-concept may be appraised; to others its value is limited to simply asking the child to point to various body parts to discover if he can differentiate left from right. The methods of evaluation used include verbal responses to directions, pointing to body parts, constructing mannequins out of disjointed body parts, drawing pictures of people, self-reporting questionnaires of various kinds, imitation of gestures, and projective tests. The application of these measures requires reasonably sophisticated subjects, who are generally not found within populations of low-level retardates.*

Using the results of assessment devices in which children were asked to respond to verbal directions, sequences appeared which offer guidelines for building the body-image at the verbal-cognitive level. The body-image, at least in a general way, seems to develop in both retardates and normals far earlier than speech and verbal comprehension. Therefore, the variety of movement experiences children have very early in their lives will contribute in subtle ways to the development of their body-image.

A recent study of concepts of body-image by Hill and others[12] involving two groups of retarded children, produced similar results for both groups although one group received training which included verbal directions coupled with left-right judgments (*i.e.,* "throw the ball with your *left* hand"), while the second group received verbal directions without any special left-right discriminations (*i.e.,* "throw the ball with *that* hand") in their movement activities which involved the use of one hand or foot.

Further evidence that movement aids the development of concepts about the body can be found in a study reported by Ilg and Ames.[14] Their study revealed that children were able to make correct left-right judgments of hands, feet, etc., and verbalized their distinction of left from right by attaching some motor function to the body part ("I eat with my right hand," "I write with my left hand," etc.).

Principles evolving from the sensory-tonic theory of perception outlined by Werner and Wapner suggest that certain alterations of bodily tonus may influence some judgments in visual space.[27]* In laboratory experiments when children's bodies were displaced in space (tilted to the left or to the right), the children's

---

*A recent summary of methods in which the body-image may be evaluated is contained in a monograph by Cratty and Sams.[8]

*A critical evaluation of this theory has been written by Howard and Templeton.[13]

12

accuracy concerning judgments in visual space was affected (*i.e.,* they reported that rods tilted to the side to which their bodies had been tilted were on a vertical plane).[27] However, as normal children get older, they are less likely to be influenced by experimental disruptions of bodily tonus.[25]

Guyette, Wapner and Weiner,[11] in their study with retardates, found that older retardates seemed *more* dependent upon alterations in bodily tonus when making perceptual judgments than were the younger subjects. Further research along this vein may reveal important causal relationships between good balance and other components of the body-image and perceptual judgments necessary in forming discriminations by retardate populations.

The child's physique seems to influence his personality traits to some degree. Kagan, for example, when using normal subjects, found that the quality of impulsiveness was more often seen in boys whose body builds lent themselves to vigorous movement (*i.e.,* they had broader chests, were shorter and more muscular). Tall narrow boys, on the other hand, seemed to be more reflective than active in nature.[15]

Generally, normal adults and children are aware of the common physique-personality stereotypes,[21] and may conform to the stereotype that best describes themselves. Investigations of personality-physique comparisons among retarded children, to my knowledge, have not been carried out. However, further research may reveal causal relationships which will, in turn, lead to more meaningful motor education programs for retarded children. Such programs will, hopefully, incorporate body-image modifications which might lead to desirable personality trait changes. Perhaps then the thin, insecure child might through exercise achieve greater self-confidence through the addition of muscle size to his vulnerable body-frame.

As the result of several studies using normal, blind, and retarded subjects, I have suggested sequences of body-image judgments. The following guidelines summarize these suggestions which may be helpful in the evaluation and training of body-image.

1. Simple judgments about parts of the face and the location and names of the limbs should constitute the initial portion of a body-image training program for retarded children. Models of the face and drawings of the child's body are recommended for use during this phase.

2. In conjunction with this initial phase, the child should be learning simple object-to-body relationships (*i.e.,* "place the box nearest your head, your feet, your side, your stomach, your back"). More difficult judgments in which the child has to re-arrange his body, and react correctly to "place your side against the wall, lie down on your back", etc. can be taught.

3. Simple directions involving body movement should be presented next which include movement of the entire body ("move to the side, forward, backward, jump up, squat down") as well as limb movements. Imitative exercises, using a teacher-model (*i.e.,* "swing your arms", "bend your knees", etc.) and a mirror are helpful in this stage.

4. The exercises in these initial three phases can be made more difficult by chaining directions together (*i.e.,* "jump down and turn around", etc.).

5. When a child's *mental age* is about six, he should be exposed to body-image activities intended to improve his knowledge of left and right. Numerous left-right things should be done including movements and pointing to body parts. The easiest activities are those in which the child remains fixed and is asked to touch various left-right body parts. Slightly more difficult judgments concern the placement of objects to the left or to the right. The most difficult are those in which the child is required to re-orient himself in various left-right ways (*i.e.*, "place your left side nearest the wall, turn to your left," etc.).[5]

6. Concurrently, the child should be taught that space has left-right dimensions which correspond to his body parts. Operational transfer from body to space should be taught (*i.e.*, "John, the letter D faces toward your right hand; stretch your hand and touch it").

7. Judgments of the left and right of another person may remain too difficult for many retardates since a *normal* child cannot be expected consistently to identify correctly the left and right body parts of another person until the age of eight or nine.

There are numerous activities available to help the retarded child gain awareness of his body size and the relative size of body parts. Kephart has suggested that doing a "seat drop" when trampolining aids a child compare his total body height to his upper body size. Drawing outlines around children as they lie on shelf paper or while standing against a blackboard, and then having the child inspect these outlines aids the formation of a more accurate awareness of his own body size. Gottsman, and others have devised tests (not usually employed with retardates) which use the selection of body silhouettes to evaluate an individual's perceptions of his own body conformations.[10]

A retardate's judgments of his body size are not usually very accurate. Aarts,[1] for example, found a positive correlation between I.Q. and the ability to recognize the size and shape of body parts. Judgments about the location of body parts, the body's left-right dimensions, bodily movements, as well as the perception of body size, therefore, should be emphasized in the body-image training program for retarded children. Upon surveying the literature, the best way in which these percepts and concepts may be incorporated by the children is through carefully sequenced movement experiences.

THE PERFORMING "SELF"

In addition to perceptions about body size and the location of body parts, another important component of the child's self-concept is related to what he can *do* with his body. Two types of approaches concerning the evaluation of a child's concept of his "performing self" have been posited. The first concerns various measures of aspiration levels which can be made concerning expected performance in a *specific task** and secondly, less exact self-report which indicate a child's

*A review of some of these studies using motor performance measures may be found in Social Dimensions of Physical Activity, Chapter III, Aspiration Level[7] (Prentice-Hall, Inc. 1967).

general feelings about himself in a variety of performance situations ("Are you clumsy?") may be collected.

In general, studies of aspiration levels which use normal subjects compare estimates of performance with actual performance on trials of a given task. The findings from these studies usually confirm these common observations: (a) subjects with a background of success tend to aspire to better performance; (b) continued failure elicits low estimates of future performance; (c) insecure individuals over-react to failure and to success (*i.e.*, aspiring too high after doing well, and too low after performing poorly).

Retardates, like the insecure, may be similarly expected to take failures too hard and become elated with even minimal successes. Zeaman and Orlando, whose study has been previously discussed (Chapter 2, page 12), reported that after failure experiences, retardates could not or would not perform tasks which were previously easy for them. The studies of Oliver indicate ways in which academic aspiration may be influenced by positive feelings engendered in physical activity programs.[28]

I have used a survey form of self-reports in a general way to assess thirteen retardates' opinions of their motor performance and physical appearance.* This form is not recommended unless the child's mental age is seven or eight. A score is obtained by the children's yes-no answers to such questions as "are you clumsy?", "are you the last to be chosen in games?", and "are you good at making things with your hands?" (See Appendix, page 223). It has been found that:

1. The questions most likely to elicit responses indicating a negative self-concept on the part of the retarded children prior to a program of motor education lasting five weeks were "Do your friends make fun of you?" (answered yes by 73 per cent), and "Do you have trouble making friends?", "Do girls (boys) like you?", and "Do you play with younger children a lot?" 47 per cent of the children answered these indicating a negative self-concept, *i.e.*, does not consider himself handsome, has trouble making friends, the opposite sex does not like him, and plays with younger children a lot.

2. Following a five-month program of motor training, the children indicated as a group a significant shift toward a more positive self-concept in statements numbered 4, 6, 8, and 20 (See Appendix, page 223), indicating feelings about the way they look, their appearance, school, and reading. Their answers to the other statements on the questionnaire indicated no significant shift in the post-test.

These data make it questionable as to whether such a direct verbal assessment of self-concept is appropriate for use with retarded children. At the same time, the data collected suggested that clinicians working with retarded children, attempting to improve their self-image through movement, place emphasis upon *teaching* the children that they have improved, and making them aware in very concrete and obvious ways of the amount of improvement they have made.

Most important to retardates is the skill with which they can *do* something since they do not *think* well. The feelings they have about their physical perform-

---

*A modification short-form of the test developed by Piers and Harris.[17] Mean age of the EMR's was 8.80 (SD – 1.90); 12 were boys, 2 were girls. (Appendix C.)

ance are likely to exert positive or negative influences upon their total self-concept. It is important, then, if possible, to survey the retardates' general and specific feelings about his potential to perform a number of tasks prior to devising a program of motor training and/or physical education.* Sometimes this evaluation can be carried out in a relatively simple manner by asking a child how far he can execute a standing broad jump prior to the actual jump, and then asking for further estimates of performance from the child after the first trial. If the child refuses to guess or makes a gross over-estimate, it may be assumed that there is a considerable distortion in his self-concept. Moreover, if the child refuses to adjust to reality, there is cause for concern (*i.e.*, after an under-or-over-estimation, he refuses to be influenced by the distance jumped on the previous performance trial, when making his next estimate). A child whose self-concept of his performance potential is extremely low must be placed initially in situations in which he receives continual success experiences, whereas a child whose opinion of his performance potential is not extremely low may be challenged to a greater degree.

GAME CHOICE

Several measures of children's choice of preferred games have been used in research. At times, these studies claim to measure gender identification in children. One of the measures most frequently used in research studies was developed by Rosenberg and Sutton-Smith.[22] I used shortened modification of the test involving this measure to evaluate the vigor of the activities children preferred prior to and following a program of motor education conducted at University of California, Los Angeles. In addition, norms were obtained from a school district using 750 children from grades 2 through 5. The short-form of the Sutton-Smith test was also compared to scores obtained from a similar measure of activity choice purporting to evaluate the same attributes. Below is a survey of the findings of this research.

1. As the children grew older, they tended to select fewer games. For example, the boys and girls in the 2nd grade selected from 16 to 18 games from a list they liked to play. When the children in the 4th and 5th grades were polled, however, they proved to be more selective and chose on the average from 7 to 8 games.

2. A survey of the weighted scores given to the various games revealed significant differences between the scores elicited from both sexes by the 2nd grade (seven year olds). (These norms are found in the Appendix, page 222). It might be assumed that boys with motor problems tend to withdraw from vigorous activities. The retarded male may withdraw from vigorous activities since he cannot acquire the complex rules required. If he does participate, he may display problems of social adjustment and undue aggression in game situations with normal children because of the frustration involved.[26]

A comparision was made of the number and type of games selected by normal children as compared to those collected from retardates. The results of these comparisons are:

1. There was a significant difference between the weighted masculine scores

---

*It may be found that a considerable difference exists between actual performance measured and the child's feelings about his performance.

elicited from 13 retarded boys (mean = 33.08, SD = 11.34), and the scores elicited from 82 average nine year olds (mean = 23.64, SD = 12.08) (t = 2.66).

2. On the other hand, it appears as if the two girls showed a tendency to choose more masculine games as their scores based upon the boy-like games averaged 19.50 (SD = 6.50). Whereas the norms for this type of score are 9.60 (SD = 15.78). However, there are too few subjects, of course, to draw any valid inferences from these data. The scores elicited from the more feminine games from this test from the two girls averaged 45.50 which is similar to the norm for nine-year-old girls of 30.42.

3. The retarded boys chose 13.55 "masculine games" as compared to the average score of 10.27 games chosen by a population upon which this test was normed.

4. The girls, on the other hand, chose 15 feminine games on the list, as compared to an average of 10 games chosen by average children upon which the test was normed.

Results of other studies in which game measures have been utilized in children are as follows:

1. Boys and girls' game choices tend to be similar until the age of seven and eight, at which time the girls tend to choose more passive activities, and the boys more active ones.

2. In the past, girls in America have tended to evidence an increased tendency to select vigorous games at earlier ages. This conclusion is based upon comparisons of game choices taken at twenty-year intervals.[23]

3. Game choice is only one of the indices that incorrect gender identification may be occurring in a given child. Other indices include the inclination to use gestures of a member of the opposite sex, the expression of the desire to be a member of the opposite sex, and dressing like a member of the opposite sex.

4. As a child matures, he tends to become more selective when confronted with lists of games; he tends to engage in fewer games as he grows older.

Children's behavior patterns tend to be transmitted from one child to another. Thus it is possible that a boy, refused participation in vigorous games, may play with girls and select the more passive games associated with them, and as a result, imitate their gestures and other movement characteristics. Although there are no definitive studies concerning this point of which I am aware, it is apparent to many educators upon observing groups of retarded boys that they manifest excessive silly behavior. It is possible that the introduction of vigorous activity, accompanied by specific training in movement patterns which are generally seen among boys (vigorous striking with a fist, a wide base when running, etc.), might result in better acceptance of retardates by their normal peers in play activities.

SUMMARY

A child's total feelings about himself include both obvious and subtle components of his personality, some of which relate to, or are influenced by motor activity and motor attributes. This chapter discussed some of these components including the body-image, body-size, general self-confidence in motor activity, and aspiration level in specific tasks and game choice. That which is important to a child is not how well he actually performs, but what he *feels* about his performance after it is completed, and what he chooses to do next. Adequate insight as to the importance of these feelings to the children is essential to improving the development of the atypical children through motor activity.

REFERENCES

1. Aarts, J. F. M. C.: "Some Experiments on The Accuracy of Self-Judgements," *Arto. Psychol.; 25,* 137–158, 1966.
2. Adams, N. and Caldwell, W.: "The Children's Somatic Apperception Tests," *J. Gen. Psychol.; 68,* 43–57, 1963.
3. Bérges, J. and Lézine, L.: *The Imitation of Gestures,* The Spastics Society Medical Education and Information Unit Association, London, William Heinemann, Medical Books Ltd., 1965.
4. Clausen, Johannes: *Ability Structure and Subgroups in Mental Retardation,* Washington, Spartan Books, 1966.
5. Cratty, Bryant J.: *Developmental Sequences of Perceptual-Motor Tasks: Movement Activities for Neurologically Handicapped and Retarded Children and Youth,* Freeport, L.I., New York, Educational Activities, Inc., 1967.
6. ———: *Perceptual-Motor Attributes of Mentally Retarded Children and Youth* (Monograph), Los Angeles County Mental Retardation Services Board, 1966.
7. ———: *Social Dimensions of Physical Activity,* Englewood Cliffs, New Jersey, Prentice-Hall, Inc., 1967.
8. Cratty, Bryant J. and Sams, Theressa: *The Body-Image of Blind Children* (Monograph), Sponsored by the American Foundation For the Blind, New York, 1968.
9. Gallagher, James J.: "Measurement of Personality Development in Pre-Adolescent Mentally Retarded Children," *Am. J. Ment. Defic.; 64,* 296–384, Sept., 1959.
10. Gottesman, Eleanor and Brown, L. W.: "The Body-Image Identification Test: A Quantitative Propeture Technique to Study as Aspect of the Body-Image," *J. Genet. Psychol.; 108,* 19–34, 1966.
11. Guyette, A., Wapner, Seymour, Werner, Heinz, and Davidson, John: "Some Aspects of Space Perception in Mental Retardates," *Am. J. Ment. Defic.; 69,* 90–100, July, 1964.
12. Hill, S. D., McCullum, A. A., and Sceau, A.: "Relation of Training In Motor Activity to Development of Left-Right Directionality In Mentally Retarded Children: Exploratory Study," *Percept. & Mot. Skills; 24,* 363–366, 1967.
13. Howard, I. P., and Templeton, W. B.: *Human Spatial Orientation,* New York, John Wiley & Sons, 1966.
14. Ilg, Frances L. and Ames, Louise Bates: *School Readiness,* New York, Harper & Row, 1965.
15. Kagan, Jerome: "Body Build and Conceptual Impulsivity in Children," *J. Person.; 34,* 118–128, 1966.
16. Oliver, J. N.: "The Effect of Physical Conditioning Exercises and Activities on The Mental Characteristics of Educationally Sub-Normal Boys," *Br. J. Ed. Psychol.; 28,* 155–165, June, 1958.
17. Piers, Ellen V., and Harris, Dale B.: "Age and Other Correlates On Self-Concept In Children," *J. Ed. Psychol.; 55,* April, 1964.
18. Rosenberg, B. G., and Sutton-Smith, B.: "The Measurement of Masculinity and Femininity In Children," *Child. Devel.; 30,* 373–380, 1959.
19. ———: "A Revised Conception of Masculine-Feminine Differences in Play Activities," *J. Genet. Psychol.; 96,* 165–170, 1960.

20. Secord, Paul F., and Jourard, Sidney, M.: "The Appraisal of Body-Cathexis: Body-Cathexis and the Self," *J. Consult. Psychol.; 17,* 343–347, 1953.

21. Sleet, David A.: "Somatotype and Social Image," Paper presented at the Annual Meeting of the California Association of Health, Physical Education, and Recreation; San Jose, California, April 8, 1968.

22. Sutton-Smith, and Rosenberg, B. G.: *Play and Game List,* Bowling Green, Ohio: Bowling Green State University, 1959.

23. ———: "Sixty Years of Historical Changes in the Game Preferences of American Children," *J. Am. Folkl.; 74,* 17–46, 1961.

24. Sutton-Smith, B., Rosenberg, B. G., and Morgan, E. F.: "Development Of Sex Differences in Play Choices During Pre-Adolescence," *Child Devel.; 34,* 119–126, 1963.

25. Wapner, Seymour and Heinz, Werner: *Perceptual Development: An Investigation Within The Framework of Sensory Tonic Field Theory,* Clark University Press, 1957.

26. Weatherford, R. S. and Harrocks, John: "Peer Acceptance and Over and Under Achievement In School," *J. Psychol.; 66,* 215–220, 1967.

27. Werner, Heinz and Wapner, W.: "Sensory-Tonic Field Theory of Perception," *J. Person.; 18,* 88–107, 1949.

28. Zeaman, D. and House, Betty J.: "The Role of Attention In Retardate Discrimination Learning," In *Handbook of Mental Deficiency,* N.R. Ellis (Ed.), New York, McGraw-Hill Book Co., 159–223, 1963.

11

Games with Ideas

Most children like to play games, particularly if the games involve total movement of the body through space. To an increasing degree, games of this nature are being utilized as channels through which children learn concepts and skills usually associated with the classroom. Jim Humphrey[9] at the University of Maryland has demonstrated that better learning of verbal skills and of arithmetic concepts occurred with some children when they were taken to the playground where mathematical and verbal skills were incorporated into their games than was achieved when using the traditional workbooks.

Schools for special education in the City of Los Angeles have added lines and configurations to the patterns usually found on the playground with the intention to use total body movement as a learning modality in addition to the visual, auditory, and tactual channels ordinarily relied upon. While this method of instructing concepts and classroom skills has several advantages, it is not my intention to imply that traditional methods should be replaced by the so-called learning-games.

There are several reasons why movement as a learning modality holds promise for the education of children with learning dificulties, one of which is the strong motivation attached to it. Game performance is a motivating device for many children because the results of their activity are immediate and concrete. It is instantly rewarding for a child to spell a word correctly in some game situation in the classroom or on the playground so that he can proceed to the next base. While movement as a learning modality may not be essential for all children, a study directed by Petri[13] supports the idea that movement can help some children learn.

According to Petri, children deal with their environment in two ways. Some children explore their environment through total body movement, and this group was labeled the reducer of stimuli. The second group tends to be very inactive physically, and these children were called the augmenters of stimuli. The reducer prefers moving about in his environment, rather than sitting quietly and perceiving the activity about him. He tends to be less sensitive to pain. Further, because of his activity, he tends to inhibit the input of sensory experiences. The augmenter manifests a tendency to absorb information passively and is less inclined to movement. This type of child tends to be more sensitive to his environment and to pain.

If Petri's hypothesis is accepted, then it would seem that both active and passive learning activities should be included in schools. The augmenter is receptive to regular classroom teaching techniques, the reducer seems to need a different approach to learning. One type of child, then, learns through passively perceiving his environment, while the other needs movement.

Total movement may better demonstrate the quality of a child's thought processes to the observing teacher than will more subtle performance on desk-top tasks. The difficulty of tasks described on the following pages may be easily altered; large stimuli are being reacted to and most of these stimuli may be changed continually to make the tasks challenging.

While many children learn easily and readily respond to audio-visual stimuli, some very vigorous boys need a different approach to learning, one in which body movements stimulate the learning process. The boy who attempts to assert his masculinity by engaging in frequent movement may be more amenable to more vigorous learning methodologies than to the passive classroom tasks having a feminine connotation taught by his feminine teacher. Kagan,[11] for example, found that with the possible exception of mathematics, most classroom tasks such as reading and writing are felt to be feminine by boys in the elementary school. Movement tasks oriented toward the acquisition of concepts needed in the classroom may help a hyperactive child improve his motor problems. Well-designed movement tasks may help boys develop self direction and control.

Several classifications of concepts which may be improved through movement activities are discussed in this chapter. Included are tasks purporting to enhance serial memory ability, the recognition of and discrimination between geometric patterns, choice-making behavior, and the ability to classify. Games on grids containing letters and numbers are taught the children as a means of developing spelling and arithmetic skills, as well as simple letter and number recognition. Base games arranged in order of difficulty conclude this section.

SERIAL MEMORY ABILITY

Serial memory ability is a basic learning attribute. The correct arrangement of letters into words, words into phrases, and the ability to recall a series of instructions in correct order are vital qualities for a child to possess. A close relationship exists between the ability to remember a series of stimuli and the ability to assimilate a number of stimuli at a single exposure or a perceptual-span. There are several hypotheses which attempt to explain how components in a series are remembered.[10] Some studies suggest that one item seems to trigger the next item in a series; other research states that the location of a given item in a series is important, while a third assumption suggests that both these processes interact to aid children remember things in a series and to place them in correct order.

Relating to these projects in serial memory ability, the findings of two studies by Cratty have demonstrated that the nature of serial learning of words is similar to the manner in which a series of movements are learned and retained.[2,5]

Movement activities which may be used to heighten serial memory ability are as follows.

1. A single child may watch another child execute the series of movements and then: (*a*) he may attempt to imitate the series himself (a fairly difficult task); (*b*) he may instruct a third child on the manner in which the first child moved through the various configurations (easier than the first sub-problem recommended).

2. The instructor may add to the number of "movement items" a given child must do or attempt to imitate. With trainable retardates, it is best to start with one, then move to two, and later to three and four movement sub-tasks; the educable and many normal youngsters can perform five, six, and even seven. To recall more than six or seven usually requires reasonably high intelligence.

3. Serial memory tasks of the preceding nature may be combined with instructions which encourage the development of other perceptual and conceptual attributes concurrently. For example, these configurations may consist of geometrical figures, of letters, or of combinations of figures and letters. Children seem to find it easier to identify larger geometric figures than smaller ones. Therefore, they can more readily recall the items in a serial memory task if the larger letters and figures are used than to try to identify the smaller letters of a printed page in their books. To stimulate the reader to try some of these learning activities with certain children, a few suggestions are offered.

A child may be asked to perform some activity to one or more of the patterns, or he may be asked to identify verbally the type of pattern encountered, before proceeding to do some movement within it, over it, or around it. The children who are watching may be asked to call out each geometric shape encountered by the performer as he reaches it.

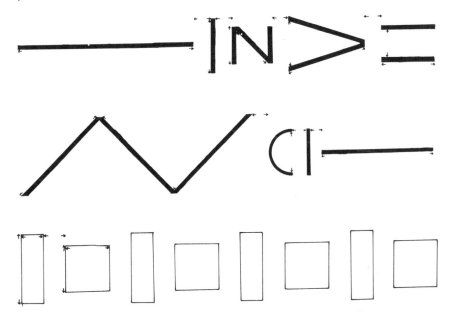

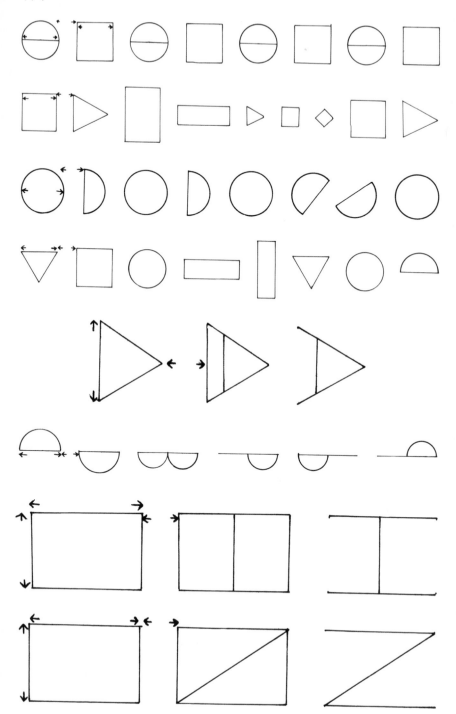

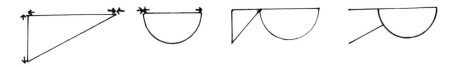

Various kinds of cross-modal transfer problems may be worked out in this situation if a child, for example, is asked to draw each figure he encounters in the serial task on an adjacent blackboard.[14]

Pattern sequences may contain both lines and geometric figures placed in order. In the following diagram, when a child walks the line (1), dynamic balance is aided; when he jumps over the next line (2), visual-motor coordination is required, and when he copies another child in these two movements, serial memory ability is involved. When he encounters the triangle, he may be asked, "What is it?" before being asked to jump into it with his left foot first (pattern recognition and left-right discrimination); and as he gets to the final square, he may be asked to perform in four ways in using the square (response generalization and decision making is left up to him).

Using the same series of patterns, place one child at each of the four patterns. Ask each child to do four or more movements on, around, or in his pattern. Each of these four performers may be observed by four other children who evaluate their efforts and keep score. Many teachers, after they have given the children a problem to solve, fail to give the children sufficient time to think about what they want to do within the limits of the assigned task. Too frequently teachers expect an immediate response to the assigned problem.

If materials are available, such as obstacle course may be constructed of tires, boxes, and other materials which encourage a child to work in a third dimension, height. As soon as the children are able to engage in decision making behavior, they should be encouraged to construct their own obstacle course using tape and other available objects.

PATTERN RECOGNITION

In Chapter 3 the idea of the lesson in triangles was discussed. If the triangles were observed, touched, and talked about so that some triangular concept had been formulated, then a triangle lesson using total body movement would make use of another aspect of the child's nature to develop the concept of triangularity (*i.e.*, an enclosed space bounded by three sides, intersecting at three corners). Similar lessons in geometric figures should accompany similar movement tasks on the playground.

A few geometric figures with their dimensions are suggested below as guides to what would be appropriate to paint on a playground.

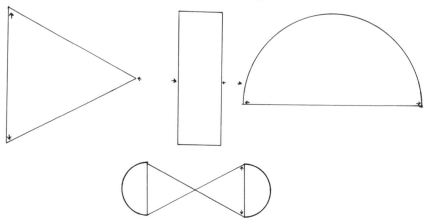

Pattern recognition training can be carried out in a number of ways.

1. Triangles cut out in the classroom may be taken to the playground so that similar patterns may be found inscribed there.

2. Children may be encouraged to trace a triangular (or square or circular) shaped pathway in a sandbox as they walk through it.

3. Various geometric figures may be drawn on a blackboard placed outside and then children may race to the corresponding figures on the playground.

4. Reasonably complex figures may be drawn on a piece of paper, and then the child may be required to walk in a similar pattern in a sandbox. Research by Keogh and Keogh indicates that some children have great dificulty organizing and fragmenting space in this way.[17] Two patterns which may be employed in this type of task are:

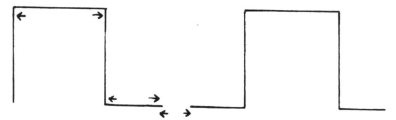

CLASSIFICATION, CATEGORIZATION

Researchers interested in cognitive processes frequently identify the ability to arrange stimuli into classifications as an important attribute underlying thought. Movement tasks properly presented may help some children to learn how to classify. Clarke and others[1] have demonstrated that this attribute is a general one, and that a remarkable amount of transfer may occur between various tasks in which different stimuli are sorted. A few suggestions may bring out other ideas.

1. To encourage children to arrange movements into categories; request them

to demonstrate ways of: (a) jumping over a line, (b) stepping over a line, (c) walking the length of a line.

2. An observing child may attempt to classify the movements of another child into categories of jumping, hopping, rolling, walking, etc., movements, as he watches him deal with the previously described line "obstacle courses" or perhaps rolling movements of various kinds using a mat.

SPELLING, ARITHMETIC

Grids (6 x 6 feet) containing 36 squares (1 x 1 foot) are a helpful way of teaching some children to spell and to handle various simple numerical concepts. The immature child, the child who resists traditional ways of teaching these skills, as well as the vigorous, muscular boy who is more likely to be hyperactive, are all receptive to these kinds of tasks.[11]

The interior of each grid square should be large enough to contain both feet of a reasonably large child. If the size of the total grid is too large, difficulty will be incurred as the child attempts to get from letter to letter as he jumps and spells.

D	A	Y	M	S	U
X	R	U	P	B	G
B	L	K	I	H	Q
M	Z	R	E	F	O
C	O	I	V	M	T
W	D	T	P	V	E

Innumerable games may be played utilizing these squares. Care, of course, must be taken so that the child is correctly oriented to the letters and numbers and is not viewing them upside down when asked to identify them.

5	6	5	7	8	4
8	2	6	8	2	3
3	4	1	5	6	7
9	0	3	9	1	0
7	3	4	0	6	1
2	8	2	1	7	9

Grids may also contain squares with = signs, plus and minus signs and squares containing pictures of animals, etc. Thus a child can, by jumping, "say" 2 + 2 = 4; or 3 rabbits plus 4 rabbits = 7 rabbits.

1. The child may be asked to jump randomly around the squares of the grid; to identify letters or numbers by jumping on them as directed; to spell his name or various words he uses in his writing and reading vocabulary by jumping on letters in sequence.

2. The child may spell words by throwing bean bags into the lettered squares.

3. Two children may be given a single letter and asked to see who can get to the letter first.

4. Words or letters may be flashed to the children who then must duplicate the order by jumping or hopping into the proper squares containing the same words or letters. The same activity may be repeated with the number squares.

5. Children in adjacent squares may race to see who can spell words correctly and finish first by jumping into the appropriate squares.

6. The answers to mathematics problems may be found by having the children compute the answers by jumping into the correct squares.

Some of these activities are illustrated.

Research which invests the use of these grids in the improvement of spelling, arithmetic skills, number recognition and similar skills is presently in progress in our laboratory at UCLA.

13

BASE GAMES AND THE USE OF SPACE

Base games are popular with children of all ages. However, to participate successfully in a base game such as kickball, an elementary child must successfully integrate and "call-up", when appropriate, from 10 to 15 simple rules. It is apparent that children with learning problems, then, may not be able to participate successfully in even these low organized games because there are too many rules for them to sort out quickly.

The suggested activities illustrate ways in which base games may be introduced to the child, starting with very simple ones and moving toward those that are more complex.

Too much movement may serve to confuse a retarded child. He may become more dismayed if he is required to move too rapidly through moving objects and people. It is important that he is gradually introduced to games that demand more movement of objects and people. The initial games in the series have been selected to keep complex movements to a minimum. For example, if a retarded child is asked to run from base to base within a playfield composed of moving outfielders and the moving ball, he may well "get lost" while attempting to move from second to third base. On the other hand, if the base is placed at a point outside the usual playing field, some of this confusion is dissipated. It is easier for a child to organize the space requirements of a base game if there is no ball involved in the activity during the initial phases of learning. Therefore, the first games are played without a ball, and the child is required to find various bases and to move to them in a given order.

Playing many base games helps the child gain different attributes such as: the keeping of score which helps develop arithmetic skills, and the remembering of the order in which the bases are to be run develops the child's serial memory ability. Various dynamic properties of space and the child's ability to deal with them are learned as balls are intercepted and propelled from player to player.

The sequence of activities below is meant to offer helpful guidelines. Teachers may discover intermediate activities or may modify the games illustrated in any manner that will be helpful to the participating children.

1. 2-BASE

    One, two or more bases may be placed from 10 to 15 feet apart, and as children pass between them, or fun figure-eights around them, they can be asked to tell when their left or right side, or hand, is nearest the nearest base. Modifications can be made in the method of travel, and children can hop, jump, or skip between the bases.

2. 3-BASE TRAVELS

Using three bases placed in a triangle, children can run or move in other ways between the bases, gaining the concept of triangularity, counting bases, and generally locating the bases.

3. 4-BASE CHANGES

Beginning with four children on each of four bases, a fifth "leader" can call "change." Each child attempts to reach the next base by running, jumping, etc. before the other three can. The last child to arrive becomes "out" and a new child joins the other three to play again.

4. 3 OR 4-BASE STAND AND THROW

Using three of four bases, children may stand on each base and throw, roll, or bounce a ball around the bases. Additional stress may be imposed as another child, by running or moving in some other way, attempts to circle the outside of the bases attempting to beat the throw around, as shown in the second illustration.

5. 4-BASE THROW AND RUN TO WIN

The "up" child may kick or hit the ball to the outfield and then may attempt to circle the bases as many times as possible, passing home to first base more than once if he can. Score is kept on how many bases are touched, before the outfield can intercept the ball and stop the runner by lining up, passing the ball to the rear most man who may yell "stop."

6. 1-BASE THROW AND RUN

Using a ball the "up" child may throw, hit or kick a ball to the other children in the outfield. He can then attempt to circle the single base as many times as he can, counting his attempts, before the outfielders can "stop" him by intercepting the ball, lining up behind each other, passing the ball to the rear man who yells "stop" to terminate the actions of the "up" man.

7. 1-BASE CIRCLE YOUR TEAMMATES

After hitting, throwing or kicking the ball, the up man circles his own teammates, while the outfielders all react by lining up behind the man intercepting it, passing it to the rear man who yells "stop" to stop the runner. Activities of this nature in which all of the players have to do something most of the time are helpful in so far as there is less probability that the immature or distractible child will remove his attention from the game situation.

8. 2-BASE HIT AND TRAVEL

The up man kicks, hits or throws the ball, and then travels to the 2nd base which is in a direction *opposite* to that in which the outfielders are located. The outfielders attempt to return the ball home or line up and yell "stop" as described in the previous games before the up man can return to home base again. Two players up can also be used, so that the first player does not have to return home, but may be "hit" home by the other's efforts. Traveling to bases outside the field of play is helpful insofar as confusion caused by the simultaneous movements of balls, outfielders, and base runners within the same space is reduced. There is less likely to be accidents when this type of modification is employed with retarded children.

9. 3-AND 4-BASE HIT, KICK, AND COUNT

The up player propels the ball in some manner to the outfield, and begins to run the bases continuously counting how many he can touch (he may circle them several times) before the outfield can return the ball, line up, and yell "stop", or in some other way terminate his efforts. Only one player at a time need be "up" so that waiting for a turn can be eliminated as all players are in the outfield, when not otherwise occupied. Players may be up several times and the winner is decided by the total bases traversed; thus the game affords counting and adding practice.

10. 4-BASE FORCE HOME

With five or more players on a team, players hit or otherwise propel the ball, and then just run to 1st base, moving ahead one base when their teammate hits the ball. All runs are thus forced home, and only forced outs may be made by touching a base ahead of a base runner. Three outs to a side. This modification eliminates some of the rules found in the ordinary kickball game, and at the same time lessens the chances for injury as players do not hit or tag a runner with the ball.

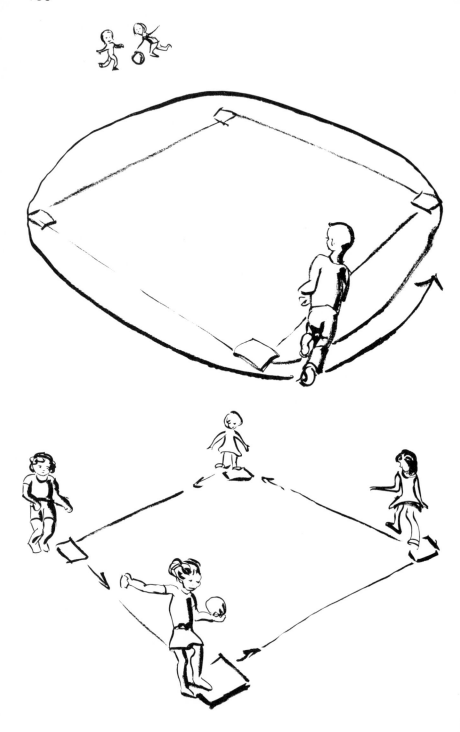

If and when these games are mastered, the child may be ready for standard games such as kickball. At times, if the teacher attempts to change from game to game too rapidly, negative transfer will occur (*i.e.*, the rules of the previous game will interfere with the learning of subsequent games). It is well to spend some time with a single game and its modifications prior to moving to a second game, particularly if the children involved evidence marked learning problems.

SUMMARY

The learning games outlined on the preceding pages are not presented as ways to replace traditional learning techniques, but as helpful adjuncts to these. The creative teacher should be able continually to make modifications to the tasks outlined if the principles underlying these activities are thoroughly understood.

Activities of this type are a helpful way of observing the quality of a child's thought processes. At various points during the performance of these kinds of skills, the teacher should permit, indeed should encourage, silent contemplation of the elements of the task the child is trying to organize. Sometimes, particularly in the case of the severely retarded, the time required prior to some decision being made may be prolonged indeed. The teacher should attempt to control her own anxieties during this apparently inactive period of time, for what could be more gratifying to a teacher or a parent than to watch a retarded child think.

REFERENCES

1. Clarke, Ann, Cooper, G. M. and Henney, A. S.: "Width of Transfer and Task Complexity in the Conceptual Learning of Imbeciles", *Br. J. Psychol.; 57,* 121–128, 1966.
2. Cratty, Bryant J.: "Comparison of Verbal-Motor Performance and Learning in Serial Memory Tasks", *Res. Quart.; 34,* 431–439, December, 1964.
3. ———: *Learning and Playing: 50 Vigorous Games for Atypical Children,* Freeport, New York, Educational Activities, Inc., 1968.
4. ———: "Moving and Learning", Chapter XI, in Developmental Sequences of Perceptual-Motor Tasks, Freeport, New York, Educational Activities, Inc., 1967.
5. ———: "Recency vs. Primary in a complex Gross Motor Task", *Res. Quart.; 34,* 3–8, 1963.
6. Ghent, L., and Bernstein, L.: "Effect of Orientation on Recognition of Geometric Forms by Retarded Children", *Child, Devel.; 35,* 1127–1136, 1963.
7. Gibson, E. J., Gibson, J. J., Pick, A. and Oseer, H. A.: "A Developmental Study of the Discrimination of Letter-Like Forms", *J. Comp. Phys. Psychol.; 55,* 897–907, 1962.
8. Hill, S. D., McCullum, A. H. and Sceau, A.: "Relation of Training In Motor Activity to Development of Left-Right Directionality in Mentally Retarded Children: Exploratory Study", *Percept. & Mot. Skills; 24,* 363–366, 1967.
9. Humphrey, James H.: "Comparison of the Use of Active Games and Language Workbook Exercises as Learning Media in the Development of Language Understandings With Third Grade Children", *Percept. & Mot. Skills; 21,* 23–26, 1965.
10. Jensen, Arthur R. and Rolnver, D. Jr.: "What is Learned in Serial Learning?", *J. Verbal Behavior; 4,* 62–72, 1965.
11. Kagan, J., Wright, J. C. and Bayley, N.: "Psychological Development of the Child", Chapter 12 in *Human Development* Frank Falkner (Ed.), Philadelphia, W. B. Saunders Co., 1966.

12. Keogh, Barbara, K. and Keogh, Jack F.: "Pattern Copying and Pattern Walking Performance of Normal and Educationally Subnormal Boys", *Am. J. Ment. Defic.; 71,* 1009–1013, 1967.

13. Petri, Asenath: *Individuality in Pain and Suffering,* Chicago, University of Chicago Press, 1967.

14. Pick, Ame D., Pick, H. and Thomas, Margaret: "Cross-Model Transfer and Improvement of Form Discrimination: *J. Exp. Child. Psychol.; 3,* 279–288, 1967.

15. Roger, Fred L.: "Sequential Complexity and Motor Response Rates," *J. Exp. Psychol.; 74,* 199–202, 1967.

16. Swink, Joy, Trimbo, Don, and Noble, Merrill: "On the Length Difficulty Relation in Skill Performance," *J. Exp. Psychol.; 74,* 356–362, 1967.

Appendixes

Appendix A.

Six-Category Gross-Motor Test*

Averages, Scoring, Administrative
Procedures and Research Findings

*From Cratty, B. J.: Perceptual-Motor Behavior and Educational Processes. Springfield, Charles C Thomas Publisher, 1969.

TABLE 1: *Six-category gross-motor test*

ADMINISTRATION AND SCORING

LEVEL I—Test 1 *BODY PERCEPTION*

Equipment: 4 x 6 foot mat

Preparation: The child should be placed, standing on the floor, with his toes against the mid-point of the 4-foot edge of the mat. The tester should stand next to the child, with his feet on the floor.

General Consideration: The tester should describe and then demonstrate each movement, and then arise from the mat permitting the child to respond. The child should arise after each request and stand at the starting point described above. The child should be told "thank you" after attempting each movement.

Testing:

a. "_____(name)_____, please lie down on the mat like this on your front or stomach." (Tester then lies on his stomach, his head away from the child, remains for two seconds, arises, and says . . .) "Now try to do it too." Point is given if the child lies on his stomach regardless of whether or not head is turned away from or toward the tester.

b. "_____(name)_____, now please lie down on the mat like this on your back." (Tester lies down slowly on his back, head away from the child, remains for two seconds, arises and then says, "now try to do it too."

c. "_____(name)_____, now please lie down on the mat like this on your front or stomach, with your legs nearest me." (Tester assumes lying position, with his legs nearest the child, arises and then says . . .) "Now try to do it too." The tester should then go to the far end of the 4-foot side of the mat, and face the child with the mat between them. Point is awarded only if feet are nearest the tester, and child is on his stomach.

d. "_____(name)_____, now please lie down on the mat on your side, like this . . ." (Tester lies down on his left side, feet toward the child, arises, and then says . . .) "Now try to do it too." Point is awarded no matter which side the child chooses to lie upon, nor where the feet are relative to the tester.

e. The tester should then say, "Now let me see you lie down on your left side." This should *not* be demonstrated. A 5th point is awarded in this category if the child correctly lies on his left side.

Scoring: One point is given for correctly executing each of the following requests. No points are deducted for a slowly executed response. Total of 5 points possible.

LEVEL I—Test 2 *GROSS AGILITY*

Equipment: 4 x 6 foot mat; stop-watch

Preparation: Child is asked to stand in the center of the mat, facing a 4-foot side and the tester. Tester should be 10 feet away. Then the child should be asked to lie down in the middle of the mat, his feet toward the tester.

Instructions: After the child is in the above position, the tester should say, "I would like to see how fast you can stand up and face me." A stop-watch should be started as the child's head leaves the mat, and stopped as he has his knees straight as he assumes a standing position, facing the tester. If the child does not understand, the tester should demonstrate standing up rapidly.

Scoring: 1 point if the child turns to his stomach first and then arises in more than three seconds.

2 points if the child turns to his stomach first and arises under three seconds.

3 points if the child sits up, without turning over, and stands up without turning his back to the tester taking more than three seconds.

4 points if the child sits up, remains facing the tester when arising, and does so in two seconds.

5 points if the child sits up, remains facing the tester when arising, and does so under two seconds.

Note: A second hand on the standard watch may be used in lieu of a stop-watch. Maximum points possible, 5.

LEVEL 1—Test 3 *BALANCE*

Equipment: Stop-watch

Preparation: The tester should face the child on a level floor ten feet away.

Instructions: After getting the child in this position the tester should say . . . "I would like to see how long you can stand on one foot like this" . . . (the tester should demonstrate balancing on his left foot, using his arms to assist him and should then say . . ." Now you try it too." (Tester should demonstrate the held position for ten seconds.)

Scoring: 1 point if attempted and held for one second.
2 points if attempted and held from two to 4 seconds.
3 points if attempted and held from four to six seconds.
4 points if attempted and held over 6 seconds.

Second part: "Now let's see if you can balance on one foot with your arms folded, like this." (Tester should demonstrate by posturing on one foot with arms folded across his chest for ten seconds.)

Scoring: 5 points in this test if arm-folded balance is held from three to four seconds. Maximum 5 points possible.

Permit the child to remain balanced on both parts of this test for ten seconds, and then suggest that he stop. The scoring is not influenced by the foot he decides to balance upon, however, it should be the same foot throughout.

LEVEL I—Test 4 LOCOMOTOR AGILITY

Equipment: 4 x 6 foot mat

Preparation: Ask the child to stand on the floor, with his feet touching the mat in the middle of one of its 4-foot sides. The tester should place himself at the same end.

Instructions: After the child is in place, the tester says . . .

a. "_____(name)_____, let's see if you can crawl across the mat like this," (tester crawls on hands and knees in the correct pattern down the length of the mat away from the child, then toward the child, and then the tester says), "Now you try it too." One point scored if a correct cross-extension pattern is seen in the crawling movement.

b. "_____(name)_____, let's see now if you can walk down the mat like this," (tester walks down the mat away from the child and then says), "Now let's see if you can do it too." Additional point is scored if cross-extension pattern is seen in gait.

c. "___(name)___, now can you jump a cross the mat like this?" (tester takes three to four jumps across the mat, using both feet together and proper arm lift as he travels and then says), "Now you try too." One point is scored if the child leaves the ground two to three times during trip down the mat.

d. "___(name)___, now let's see you jump backwards down the mat like this." (tester jumps backwards toward the child and then says), "Now let me see you do it." A point is given if the child can jump backwards two to three times without falling down, proceeding down the mat. He is permitted to look behind himself when executing this test. Tester should return to the far end of the mat and await the child, stop him and prevent him from falling on the floor as he completes his trip.

e. "___(name)___, now let's see you hop down the mat on one foot like this," (tester demonstrates one foot hopping, using his left foot across the mat away from the child and then says), "Now let me see you do it." One additional point is scored if child is able to hop on one (either one) from two to three times down the mat.

Maximum 5 points possible.

LEVEL I—Test 5 *BALL THROWING*

Equipment: Rubber playground ball, 8 inches in diameter

Preparation: Ball is placed at the child's feet, tester faces the child, 15 feet away.

Testing: The child is asked to pick up the ball and throw it to the tester. The tester should say, "___(name)___, please pick up the ball and throw it to me." (The tester should then execute a proper one-handed overhand throwing movement.) And at the same time should say, "Like this." The ball is rolled back to the child, and he should be permitted five throws.

Scoring: 1 point is given if he pushes the ball with his hands or feet.

2 points are given if he throws the ball, either overhand or underhand using both arms at the same time.

3 points are given if the ball is thrown with one arm without any body shift into the throw.

4 points are given if the child throws with a weight shift forward of the body, without proper step on the opposite foot.

5 points are given if the child throws with a weight shift at the time the ball is released, and with a step with the opposite foot occurring at the same time.

Give the child the proper score based upon the habitual way he selected to throw the ball, *i.e.*, the manner in which he throws it three out of five times. Maximum 5 points possible.

LEVEL I—Test 6 *BALL TRACKING*

Equipment: 8½ inch rubber, air-filled playground ball

Preparation: The child should face the tester 10 feet away. The tester should hold the ball.

Testing: The tester should then say, "Now I will bounce the ball to you. Try to catch it any way you can." (The tester then throws the ball, so that it bounces once before the child gets it. The ball should bounce, so that it comes chest high to the child. Two practice bounces are permitted to allow the child and tester to become oriented to the problem.) The tester should then say, "Now do you understand? Catch it any way you can, with one or two hands."

Five throws should then be made to the child, bouncing the ball once. The ball may be returned by the child, any way he sees fit. About 5 seconds should be permitted between throws.

Scoring: Score 1 point for each time the ball is caught and controlled by the child. Maximum 5 points possible.

LEVEL II—Test 1 *BODY PERCEPTION*

Equipment: 4 x 6 foot mat

Preparation: The child is asked to lie on his back in the center of the mat, with his feet pointed toward the 4 foot end; the tester should stand at this end.

Testing: The tester should say . . . _____(name)_____ , now I am going to ask you to do certain things with your arms and legs, please try to do them as quickly and as accurately as you can. First close your eyes . . .'' Then the tester should say

1. ''Raise your left arm in the air.'' Then the tester should wait until the child makes a decision and moves. Then the tester says, ''Put your arm down now . . .''

2. The tester should then say, ''Raise your left leg up.'' The tester should wait until the leg is decided upon and moved and then say, ''Put your leg down now . . .''

3. The tester should then say, ''Raise your right arm in the air.'' The tester should wait until the child selects an arm and raises it and should then say, ''Put your arm down now.''

4. The tester should then say, ''Touch your left elbow with your right. ''After some movement is made, the tester should say, ''Now bring your hand down again.''

5. The tester should then say, ''Touch your right knee with your left hand.'' After these movements are completed, the tester should ask the child to open his eyes and come to his feet.

Scoring: One point is awarded for each correctly executed movement. No points are deducted for slowly executed movements. If in numbers 1 through 5, the movements are correct, but with wrong hand in every case, *i.e.* all movements backwards, a total of 3 points is awarded to the child for this test. Maximum of 5 points possible.

LEVEL II—Test 2 *GROSS AGILITY*

Equipment: 4 x 6 foot mat

Preparation: Child is placed in the center of the mat, standing and facing one of the 6-foot edges. The tester stands 10 feet away facing the child.

Tester: ''_____(name)_____ , see if you can kneel down on one knee at a time, and then stand up on one leg at a time like this without touching anything.'' (The tester then executes a four count, one to the second, movement kneeling first on one knee, then on the second, then standing on the first foot and arising on the two feet . . . the tester says then, ''Do you understand? ''Would you like to see it again?'' If the child wished to see the movement again, the tester should do so . . . and after this second demonstration, the tester should then say, ''Now you try it too.''

Scoring: 1 point is awarded if the child uses his hands on his thighs *and* on the floor to assist him in descending and/or arising.

2 points are awarded if the child touches one or both hands to his thighs when ascending and descending, or if the child comes down to both knees at once, or gets to both feet at the same time.

3 points are awarded if the child uses one or both hands while getting up only, or if he falls to one knee while arising.

14

4 points are awarded if the child executes movement without the use of the hands, but there is general unsteadiness, *i.e.* extra steps taken as the child resumes his feet, etc.

5 points are awarded if the child executes movement perfectly with the hands at the sides, not assisting the movement, and with the feet coming down and up separately.

No points are deducted if the child comes up first with a different foot from the one kneeled upon. Maximum 5 points possible.

LEVEL II—Test 3 *BALANCE*

Equipment: stop-watch

Preparation: Place the child in the standing position, on a level floor and facing away from obstacles with the tester ten feet away.

Testing: After placing the subject in the position described above, the tester should say,
  a. "I would like to see how long you can stand on one foot like this (the tester should fold his arms) with your arms folded and stand on one foot for ten seconds."
  b. If the child can accomplish this for five seconds or more, the tester should say, "I would now like you to balance on one foot like this, with your arms at your sides, and your eyes closed."
  c. If the child can accomplish this for five seconds or more, the tester should say, "I would like you to balance on one foot with your eyes closed and your arms folded like this." The tester should demonstrate with eyes closed, an arm-folded, one foot balance.
  d. If the child can accomplish this for five seconds, the tester should say, "Now try to balance on one foot with your eyes closed, arms held at your sides, but using the other foot this time." The tester should be aware of the foot preferred by the child, and request that the opposite one be used.
  e. If the child can accomplish this for five seconds, the tester should say, "Now try to balance on the same foot (non-preferred) with your arms folded and your eyes closed.

Scoring: One point is scored for each of the tests above completed successfully, *i.e.* held over five seconds. No points are given if the arms become unfolded, if they are required to be folded . . . nor if the child opens his eyes when they are required to be closed.

In each case the stop-watch should be started, or the second hand observed, as the foot leaves the ground, and stopped when it touches the next time. "Arms at your sides", means that the child can use the arms for maintaining his balance in any way that is helpful.

From ten to fifteen seconds rest should be permitted between trials. Maximum 5 points possible.

LEVEL II—Test 4 *LOCOMOTOR AGILITY*

Equipment: 4 x 6 foot mat laid out in 12 one-foot squares

Preparation: The child should face the tester at the far end of the middle of a 4-foot side. The tester should stand on the floor with his feet at the middle of the other end of the 4-foot side of the mat, facing the child.

Testing: With the child and tester in the above positions, the tester should say . . .
  a. "Now let's see if you can jump down the mat like this." (The tester then jumps two feet at a time down the mat moving straight ahead, and jumping carefully in all six squares.) The tester should then say, "Now let's see you do it . . . be sure to jump in each square and move straight ahead."
  b. After this is attempted, the tester should say, "Now let's see you jump back and forth (using only the unmarked squares so that he jumps forward with each jump) like this" . . . the tester should then say, "Now let's see you do it . . . be sure to jump only in the unmarked squares."

c. After this is attempted, the tester should say, "Now let's see you jump backwards down the mat like this." (The tester should jump directly backwards down the mat, using both feet, and landing in all six squares.) The tester should then say, "Now let's see you do it too . . . be sure to jump in all six squares." The child can be permitted to look backwards as he jumps.

d. After this is attempted, the tester should say, "Now let's see you hop down the mat like this." (The tester should then hop on the mat straight ahead, using all six squares.) The tester should then say, "Now let's see you do it. Jump in each square and move straight ahead."

e. After this is attempted, the tester should say, "Now let's see you hop down the mat like this." (The tester should then hop on one foot, hopping only in the unmarked squares, so that every hop moves him forward and from side to side.) The tester should then say, "Now let's see you do it too . . . be sure only to hop in the unmarked squares."

Scoring: One point is given for each successful trip, *i.e.* one with less than two errors in it. An error is scored when a foot(or feet) does not land in a square, when the second foot is touched, when hopping on one foot, or when an extra step is taken in a square. Maximum 5 points possible.

Ten to fifteen seconds rest should be permitted between trips. Either foot may be used for hopping, but the same foot must be used for each trip.

LEVEL II—Test 5 *BALL THROWING*

Equipment: Playground Ball 8' in diameter. 4' by 6' mat with target side up.

Preparation: The child should stand 15 feet away from the 4-foot end of the mat.

Testing: After the child has assumed the above position, the tester should stand next to him and throw the ball toward the mat's center on which is painted a 2 x 2 feet square "target"/This should be done three times . . . and the tester should then say, "I would like to take this ball and try to make it drop in the center of the mat . . . Do you understand?"

If the child is aware of the nature of the task he is permitted to throw, either overhand or underhand, with one or two hands, at the target . . . 5 times.

Scoring: 1 point is given if three attempts have hit the mat, but not the center target.
2 points are given if five attempts have hit the mat, but not the target.
3 points are given if two attempts have hit the target regardless where other throws have landed.
4 points are given if three attempts have hit the target, regardless where other throws have landed.
5 points are given if four or five throws land within the target.
The child receives *one* of the scores above *i.e.* highest score possible, 5 points.

LEVEL II—Test 6 *BALL TRACKING*

Equipment: Rubber softball hung on a string

Preparation: The tester should face the child about 2 feet away, he should ask the child to extend his arm at the shoulder, fist clenched. He should then suspend the ball on the 15-inch string so that it hangs, when motionless at the level of the child's chin (top of the ball just under the chin), and a distance away determined by the length of the child's arm plus the clenched fist.

The ball should then be suspended by the tester's left hand so that it hangs as described above. The ball should then be grasped with the tester's right hand, brought to a position which makes the string horizontal, and released so that it swings from the child's left to right in a vertical plane, parallel to the one in which the child is standing.

Testing: The tester should then permit the ball to swing back and forth in this manner 6 times and ask the child to watch it. The tester should then say, "See this ball swing back and forth? See if you can touch it with one finger like this (the tester holds the ball motionless with one hand and uses the opposite index finger on the ball touching it quickly with the tip of the opposite index finger), as it passes by you."

The tester should then hang the ball in front of the child and make sure that he starts his movement from his side, and that the touch is made directly in front of the child.

The tester should start the ball 5 times, allowing it to swing past the child 3 times after each release. As soon as the child touches it or attempts to, or the hand is extended, the ball comes back on it, and stops . . . the ball is stopped by the tester and started again.

Scoring: Score 1 point (maximum 5) for each time during each of the five sets of three swings each that the child is able to touch the ball. Make sure that no score is given if the ball touches the hand, *i.e.* as it swings back to the extended hand after a "miss" has occurred.

TABLE 2: *Average scores of normal children by age and sex on the six-category gross-motor test*

BOYS

Age	Body Perception		Gross Agility		Balance		Locomotor Agility		Throwing		Tracking		Total Battery	
	M	σ	M	σ	M	σ	M	σ	M	σ	M	σ	M	σ
(20)* 4	4.83	2.85	8.83	1.26	5.67	1.94	3.33	1.00	2.00	0.00	2.22	1.81	26.94	4.05
(22)* 5	6.12	2.54	9.56	0.80	6.60	1.20	4.36	1.92	2.16	0.78	4.24	2.06	33.00	4.99
(21)* 6	8.35	1.88	9.79	0.66	7.90	1.09	7.03	1.40	3.38	1.32	6.90	1.47	43.34	3.61
(27)* 7	9.00	1.90	9.67	1.05	8.00	1.02	7.15	1.61	5.00	1.98	7.26	1.00	46.07	3.83
(20)* 8	8.90	1.82	9.71	1.07	8.38	0.99	7.76	1.19	6.67	2.12	7.76	0.92	49.19	5.41
(23)* 9	9.65	1.11	9.70	1.10	8.60	0.86	9.05	0.97	7.15	1.93	8.10	0.62	52.40	3.69
(17)* 10	8.81	3.05	9.52	2.13	9.19	0.73	9.29	0.76	7.86	1.58	7.86	1.04	52.52	5.10
(22)* 11	9.35	2.24	9.13	2.40	9.48	0.65	9.30	1.41	8.13	2.31	8.26	1.70	53.70	7.99

Based upon scores obtained from 172 boys.
*Number of children in each group.
M = Mean

TABLE 3: Average scores of normal children by age and sex on the six-category gross-motor test

GIRLS

Age		Body Perception		Gross Agility		Balance		Locomotor Agility		Throwing		Tracking		Total Battery	
		M	σ	M	σ	M	σ	M	σ	M	σ	M	σ	M	σ
4	(18)*	4.60	1.49	6.65	2.10	4.20	1.03	5.25	1.13	4.10	1.38	3.40	2.33	28.45	5.61
5	(24)*	6.45	2.77	8.64	1.77	5.64	1.61	6.32	1.74	3.14	1.32	5.64	2.85	36.27	8.71
6	(29)*	8.38	1.81	8.33	1.91	7.00	1.63	6.29	1.27	5.24	1.33	7.05	1.56	42.29	6.46
7	(28)*	9.30	1.43	8.70	1.60	8.26	1.58	7.18	1.59	7.15	1.63	8.26	1.45	48.85	5.58
8	(21)*	9.70	0.64	9.10	1.26	8.05	1.60	9.15	0.91	8.45	1.47	8.90	0.99	53.55	4.35
9	(20)*	9.48	1.06	9.70	0.58	9.17	1.00	8.65	1.09	8.17	1.24	9.48	0.58	54.74	2.40
10	(21)*	9.82	0.71	9.88	0.47	9.23	1.26	9.23	1.06	8.88	1.08	9.82	0.38	56.71	3.80
11	(22)*	9.68	1.05	9.88	0.43	9.24	0.91	9.24	0.86	9.04	0.87	9.76	0.58	54.76	9.62

Based upon scores obtained from 183 girls.
*Number of children in each group.
M = Mean

TABLE 4: *Average scores of educable retardates by age on the six-category gross-motor test**

Age	Body Perception		Gross Agility		Balance		Locomotor Agility		Throwing		Tracking		Total Battery	
	M	σ	M	σ	M	σ	M	σ	M	σ	M	σ	M	σ
5–8	5.67	0.92	6.67	2.28	5.17	0.97	5.83	2.12	5.83	2.62	7.00	2.70	33.03	19.85
9–10	6.73	2.45	7.07	1.83	6.80	2.23	6.47	1.88	5.33	2.61	7.87	1.80	38.19	6.88
11–14	7.50	2.12	7.60	1.85	7.20	2.52	5.90	2.91	6.60	2.15	6.50	2.10	41.95	8.52
15–20	6.60	1.49	6.20	2.79	5.20	2.23	5.60	2.24	5.80	1.94	5.60	1.20	32.95	8.80

*Based upon scores obtained from 38 educable retardates.

TABLE 5: *Average scores of trainable retardates by age on the six-category gross-motor test**

Age	Body Perception		Gross Agility		Balance		Locomotor Agility		Throwing		Tracking		Total Battery	
	M	σ	M	σ	M	σ	M	σ	M	σ	M	σ	M	σ
5–6	3.18	2.33	2.50	2.13	2.43	2.42	2.35	0.91	2.29	0.90	2.62	2.29	14.42	10.06
7–8	3.21	1.46	2.56	2.72	1.95	2.01	3.25	1.90	3.11	2.16	3.20	2.34	15.96	11.88
9–10	4.53	2.55	4.52	1.70	3.24	2.45	3.77	2.88	3.25	2.25	5.59	2.89	20.65	11.93
11–12	3.33	1.68	3.09	2.25	1.76	1.92	3.45	1.69	2.85	1.68	4.47	2.79	16.30	10.78
13–14	5.38	2.51	3.76	2.79	3.61	2.90	4.15	2.66	4.07	2.02	5.61	2.03	25.78	12.82
15–16	5.40	1.50	2.15	4.70	2.80	2.64	4.20	2.52	4.20	1.99	5.30	2.33	21.20	14.19
17–20	5.87	1.92	5.12	4.10	4.37	2.40	5.12	2.10	4.25	2.34	6.00	3.39	32.12	10.28
21–24	5.57	2.20	5.14	2.57	4.42	3.90	5.00	2.28	4.14	1.25	7.33	1.90	31.19	12.54

*Based upon scores obtained from 113 trainable retardates.

TABLE 6: *Six-category gross-motor test*

CORRELATION MATRIX

		1	2	3	4	5	6	7
Body Perception	1.							
Gross Agility	2.	.32						
Balance	3.	.53	.28					
Locomotor Agility	4.	.48	.35	.62				
Throwing	5.	.52	.21	.70	.57			
Tracking	6.	.54	.36	.72	.62	.72		
Total Battery Score	7.	.73	.48	.82	.75	.81	.84	

All correlations are positive.

TABLE 7: *Factor analysis, six-category gross-motor test battery**

FACTOR I Age and General Skill	Age .57; Balance .42; Locomotor Agility .32; Ball Throw .85
FACTOR II Balance and Body Agility	Balance (Level I) .96; Balance (Level II) .79; Agility (Level I) .94; Agility (Level II) .95
FACTOR III Ball Handling, General	Locomotor Agility (Level I) .50; Ball Throwing (Level I) .52; Ball Catching (Level II) .61.
FACTOR IV Body-Perception	Body Perception (Level I) .70; Body Perception (Level II) .81; Perception, Total Score .99
FACTOR V Hand-eye, Foot-eye Coordination	Gross Agility (Total Score) .54; Locomotor Agility (Level II) .31; Ball Tracking (Level I) .57; Ball Tracking (Total) .61; Total Battery Score .46.
FACTOR VI Balance and Tracking	Balance (Level II) .39; Balance (Total) .49; Ball Tracking (Total) .35.

*Six hundred and fifty childrens' scores utilized. Taken from correlation matrix in which 19 variables were compared, including tests and sub-test scores. The Pearson Produce-Moment formula was used as a graphic representation of the data revealed linearity. The data were then subjected to a minimum residual factor analysis, using a program designed by Comrey (FORTRAN IV Program, Dept. of Psychology, UCLA, 1964). This program performed a varimax rotation of the minimum residual matrix thus the varimax matrix was the final output. Only factor loadings exceeding .3 are listed.

TABLE 8: *Comparison of six-category gross-motor test of pre-test means to post-test means, of 15 retarded children, after a five-month program of motor training**

	Pre-Test		Post-Test		t
	M	σ	M	σ	
Body Image	7.00	3.09	7.26	2.81	.53
Gross Agility	5.60	2.91	7.20	2.96	2.44*
Balance	4.46	2.40	4.73	2.35	.46
Locomotor Ability	5.46	2.23	6.53	1.86	2.55*
Throwing	3.66	2.13	4.06	1.54	.76
Tracking	6.13	3.01	7.53	2.31	2.15*
Total Score	32.13	12.68	37.66	10.65	3.74†

*Difference significant at the 5% level
† Difference significant at the 1% level
**Mean age of the group was 8.8 years, SD 1.9, 13 boys and 2 girls.

TABLE 9: *Comparison of six-category gross-motor test of pre-test means to post-test means, of 65 normal children, after a five-month program of motor training designed to remediate moderate motor problems**

	Pre-test		Post-test		t
	M	σ	M	σ	
Body Image	8.11	2.08	8.09	2.08	.08
Gross Ability	8.07	1.92	8.65	1.84	2.49†
Balance	5.48	2.29	6.39	2.59	3.81*
Locomotor Ability	6.54	1.81	7.74	2.07	5.93†
Throwing	4.30	1.82	5.04	2.25	3.43†
Tracking	6.22	2.23	7.39	2.67	3.71†
Total Score	38.74	9.21	43.33	10.36	6.02†

† = Significant at the 1% level of confidence
* = Significant at the 5% level of confidence
*Mean age of the group was 8.92, SD 2.48, there were 57 boys, 8 girls.
M = Mean

Appendix B.

Drawing Tests

Test Procedures, Norms, Scoring,
Research Results

TABLE 10: *Geometric figure drawing and conglomerate tests*

ADMINISTRATIVE INSTRUCTIONS

Equipment and Facilities:

Small room with good lighting and limited distractions, *i.e.* no posters, pictures, or toys.

Table large enough for two having a flat, *smooth* surface.

Two chairs, one of adjustable height for the child, and the other placed to the left of the child for the instructor.

Number 2 pencil without eraser is needed for the child.

Medium point, black ballpoint pens (*e.g.* Fisher Office Pen CR 64-39), are needed for the tester.

Blank sheet of paper (8 x 11) is to be used, *one* per child.

Standard Figure ditto for the child to copy.

Standard Drawing ditto (blank sheet of paper with standard drawing reversed (mirror-image) so the tester can trace from the other side). *One new ditto standard must be used for each test.*

Procedure:

Introduce yourself to the child. Then ask the child to be seated at the table. Adjust his chair so that he is in a good writing position, laterally and vertically. Place a blank sheet of paper in front of him and hand him the pencil he is to use.

The tester sits to the right of the child.

The test battery consists of two parts. The first contains five drawings. Each is to be drawn by the child on a separate sheet of paper, and each sheet of paper is held vertically by the tester as the child draws. The model is kept face down until time of use, when it is at that time placed flat in front of the child and to the top of the test sheet. The child copies the models which are to be shown in this order: CIRCLE, SQUARE, RECTANGLE, TRIANGLE, AND DIAMOND. When the child has completed each figure, the tester should mark the starting point (x), indicate the direction each line was drawn (with an arrow), and place in a separate pile face down. Directions to the child are simply: "I want you to copy this figure EXACTLY." This is stated for each figure before the child begins to draw.

When the child has finished the first part of the test, tell him: "We are now going to draw a series of figures."

The second portion of the test is made up of ten figures drawn in a series. (See sequence of figures for exact order.) Give the child one sheet of paper which is to be used horizontally. The tester obtains one standard drawing ditto for each child which is also to be placed horizontally for drawing (p. 208). The tester then draws figure one (the big square is 1). Now obtain the standard ditto and trace the second figure (the triangle in the left hand corner). Again place the standard in front of the child and to the top of the test sheet for the child to copy. Give him the same directions. When he has finished, number the starting point (this time with a 2).

This procedure is followed for all ten figures.

TABLE 11: *Sequence of figure drawing*

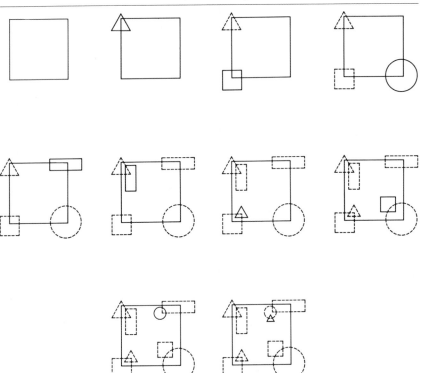

TABLE 12: *Conglomerate test*

MASTER TESTING SHEET

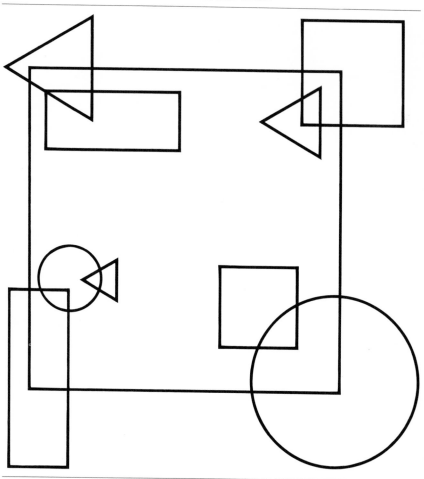

TABLE 13-A: *Geometric figure drawing test*

TEST SHEET #1

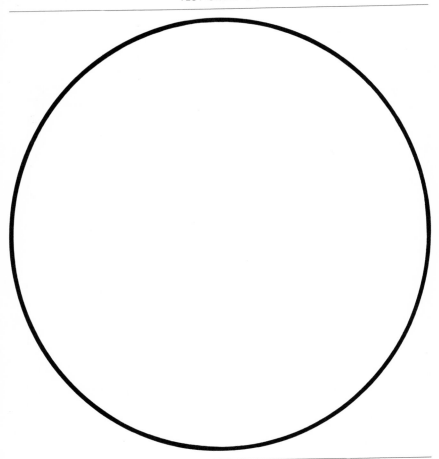

TABLE 13-B: *Geometric figure drawing test*

TEST SHEET #2

TABLE 13-C: *Geometric figure drawing test*

TEST SHEET #3

TABLE 13-D: *Geometric figure drawing test*

TEST SHEET #4

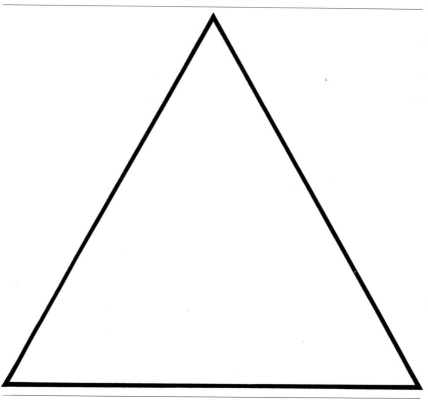

TABLE 13-E: *Geometric figure drawing test*

TEST SHEET #5

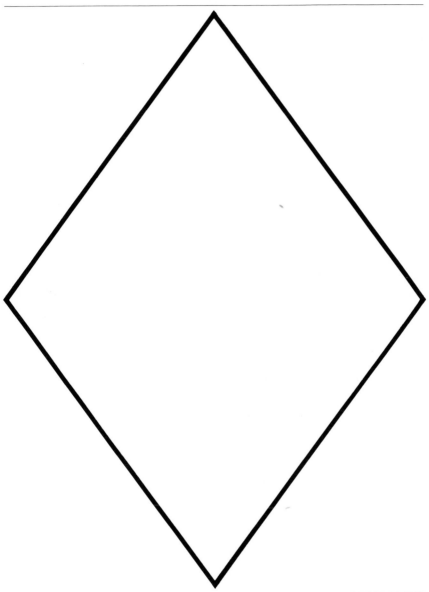

TABLE 14: *Scoring procedures, geometric figure drawing test*

Each Figure is scored separately; Two separate qualities are scored, Accuracy and Size.

ACCURACY: Each child's figure is compared to the norms on the following page, and a score is awarded each figure depending upon the norm figure, or 1, 2, or 3, to which it matches.

SIZE: Size is scored by superimposing each of the models on the corresponding figures drawn by the child. One point is scored if the child's figure is contained within the model. Two points are scored if the child's figure roughly corresponds in size to that of the model, while a score of 3 is awarded if the figure drawn by the child completely contains the model figure.

Mean of Inter-Tester Reliability = .92, based upon 40 children. Test-Re-Test reliability, based upon 40 children was as follows:

	Size	Accuracy
Circle	.95	.80
Square	.92	.78
Rectangle	.97	.82
Triangle	.95	.80
Diamond	.94	.83

TABLE 15: *Conglomerate test, scoring procedures*

ACCURACY: An accuracy score is obtained in this test by first comparing each of the figures drawn, and the first large square drawn to the scoring key on page 208, designed to assess accuracy of the individual geometric figure test. The final accuracy score on the conglomerate test is obtained by summing the accuracy scores obtained on each of the 10 figures within the final diagram and then dividing by 10.

LOCATION: A location score is obtained by scoring each of the figures drawn as either correctly placed (1) or incorrectly placed (0). To obtain a correct (1) score the smaller figure must be at the correct angle as well as at the correct location within the total diagram. Total location score possible is thus 10.

SIZE: Size is determined by superimposing the model on the child's drawing, figure by figure. If the child's figure is completely within the mode, score 1 point, if the child's drawing roughly coincides score a 2, and if the child's figure completely contains the model figure, score a 3.

Test Re-Test Reliabilities, based upon 30 children's drawings were: Size .89, Location .90 and Accuracy .81.

Inter-Observer (Scorer) reliabilities were: Size .92, Location .95 and Accuracy .82.

TABLE 16: *Geometric figure drawing test*

ACCURACY SCORING CHART

TABLE 17: *Average scores, by age, geometric figure drawing test*

Age	Circle				Square				Rectangle				Triangle				Diamond			
	Size		Accuracy		Size		Accuracy		Size		Accuracy		Size		Accuracy		Size		Accuracy	
	M	σ	M	σ	M	σ	M	σ	M	σ	M	σ	M	σ	M	σ	M	σ	M	σ
(53)*	1.0	.5	1.9	.8	1.7	.9	1.8	.5	1.4	.8	1.8	.5	1.7	.9	1.7	.6	1.4	.7	1.7	.6
(65)*	1.5	.7	2.0	.7	1.9	.9	2.0	.5	1.7	.9	1.8	.4	1.7	.9	2.0	.6	1.6	.9	1.7	.7
(47)*	1.5	.7	2.2	.7	1.5	.8	2.3	.5	1.6	.9	2.2	.5	1.6	.8	2.5	.6	1.4	.8	2.1	.6

*Number of children in each age group.
M = Mean

TABLE 18: *Average scores for 165 normal children, by age, in the conglomerate figure test*

	AGE	Size		Accuracy		Location	
		M	σ	M	σ	M	σ
(53)*	5	2.1	.9	1.1	.4	3.3	3.0
(65)*	6	2.1	1.0	1.8	.5	6.9	2.9
(47)*	7	1.6	.8	2.1	.4	9.0	1.9

*Number of children in each age group.
M = Mean

TABLE 19

		Intercorrelations Between Size and Accuracy of Childrens Drawings of Geometric Figures, Listed by Age*				
	Age	Circle	Square	Rectangle	Triangle	Diamond
(53)*	5	.03	.27	.10	.23	.02
(65)*	6	.08	.00	.01	.01	.07
(47)*	7	.12	.22	.02	.23	.06

All correlations are positive.
*Number of children in each group.

	Intercorrelations Between Size, Accuracy and Location Scores, Obtained from 165 Normal Children in the Conglomerate Figure Drawing Test		
AGE	Size-Accuracy	Accuracy-Location	Location-Size
5	.20	.45	.09
6	.11	.49	.04
7	.19	.15	.16

*based upon scores of 165 normal children.

TABLE 20: *Mean scores of conglomerate figure drawing test by 65 children participating in a motor development program, pre-and post-test comparisons.*

	Pre-Test		Post-Test		t
	M	σ	M	σ	
Size	1.62	0.61	1.82	0.57	2.04
Accuracy	9.51	5.26	9.84	5.18	1.03
Location	5.29	3.47	7.04	3.35	5.68

*Mean age of the group was 8.92 SD 2.48, 57 boys, and 8 girls.

Appendix C.

*Games Choice Test, Self-Opinion Test,
and Physical Fitness Test*

TABLE 21: *Revised Sutton-Smith games choice test*

ADMINISTRATION AND SCORING PROCEDURES

Preparation: The child should be seated to the right of the tester at the table.

General consideration: The tester should ask the question, attempting to omit in his voice inflections that may influence the child's responses. In order to establish rapport with the child the tester should ask the child whether or not he has brothers and/or sisters, and their ages. He should record these responses.

Testing:

"____(name)____, I'm going to ask you about some games. After I say the game, either you tell me 'yes' if you like to play that game, or you tell me 'no' if you do not like to play that game, or you tell me 'I don't know' if you don't know that game." (Tester then begins with the first question). "Do you like to play ____(the game)____?" (Tester waits for the child to respond and then proceeds to the next game).

Scoring:

a. General: If the child says "yes", then the tester should mark "Y" to the left of that game. If the child says "no" or "I don't know", then the tester should mark "N" to the left of that game.

b. Specific: Each game on the list has been given a weighted score by Sutton and Smith. Minimum score is 1 point, maximum score is 3 points. The weights of the "yes" responses in the boy's game category are totaled. Then the weights of the "yes" responses in the girls' game category are totaled separately. The minimum total for each category is zero points (if the child responded "no" to all the games in that category), and the maximum total for each category is 50 points (if the child responded "yes" to all the games in that category).

TABLE 22: *Revised Sutton-Smith, game choice list*

3 M 1.	Soldiers	
3 F 2.	House	
2 F 3.	Doctors	
1 M 4.	Cowboys	
3 M 5.	Hunting	
2 M 6.	Cars	
3 M 7.	Cops and Robbers	
1 M 8.	Wall Dodgeball	
2 M 9.	Marbles	
3 F 10.	Hopscotch	
3 M11.	Use Tools	
3 F 12.	Jump Rope	
3 M13.	Boxing	
1 M14.	Bowling	
2 M15.	Bandits	
3 M16.	Spaceman	
3 F 17.	London Bridge	
3 F 18.	Cooking	
2 M19.	Build Forts	

3 M20.	Toy Trains	
3 M21.	Darts	
3 F 22.	Dance	
3 M23.	Wrestling	
3 F 24.	Sewing	
3 F 25.	See Saw	
3 M26.	Football	
3 F 27.	Dolls	
3 M28.	Bows and Arrows	
3 M29.	Shooting	
3 F 30.	Jacks	
3 M31.	Make Model Airplanes	
3 F 32.	Drop the Handkerchief	
3 F 33.	Store	
3 F 34.	Farmer in the Dell	
3 F 35.	Ring Around the Rosy	
3 F 36.	Mother May I?	
3 F 37.	Musical Chairs	

TOTAL SCORES

boys' game score

girls' game score

Total Possible ____50____

Total Possible ____50____

With permission of Dr. Brian Sutton-Smith

TABLE 23: *Average scores, by sex and age, for the games-choice test*

GIRLS' MEAN SCORES

	Age	Weighted Scores				Number of Choices			
		Boys' Games		Girls' Games		Boys' Games		Girls' Games	
		M	σ	M	σ	M	σ	M	σ
(71)*	7	14.48	12.08	28.32	4.12	06.51	4.73	08.83	1.08
(71)*	8	8.97	7.02	25.53	6.13	4.14	2.92	7.13	1.72
(90)*	9	9.60	15.79	19.16	7.57	3.96	3.28	5.26	2.24
(70)*	10	7.60	8.01	15.00	6.53	3.16	2.68	4.46	1.86

*Number of children in each group.

TABLE 24: *Average scores, by sex and age, for the games-choice test*

BOYS' MEAN SCORES

Age	Weighted Scores				Number of Choices			
	Boys' Games		Girls' Games		Boys' Games		Girls' Games	
	M	σ	M	σ	M	σ	M	σ
(63)* 7	45.33	5.79	14.33	0.74	18.15	8.4	7.54	3.72
(74)* 8	36.82	10.53	9.57	6.88	15.10	7.98	6.32	4.01
(82)* 9	26.64	12.09	3.55	4.09	10.27	4.63	3.25	7.13
(83)* 10	20.77	10.44	1.71	2.59	8.08	4.26	2.96	1.01

*Number of children in each group.

TABLE 25: *Average scores by 13 retarded boys (Mean age 8.8 years) on the revised game-choice test*

	Weighted Scores				Number of Games			
	Boys' Games		Girls' Games		Boys' Games		Girls' Games	
	M	σ	M	σ	M	σ	M	σ
(13)*	33.08	11.34	28.46	14.01	13.54	4.58	10.69	6.94

TABLE 26: *Self-opinion test*

TESTING AND SCORING PROCEDURES

Preparation: The child should be seated to the right of the tester at a table.

General considerations: The tester should begin by asking the child simple questions, in order to establish rapport. The tester should then begin to ask the questions on the following page.

Testing:

'' ___(name)___ , where do you go to school?'' (The tester listens to the response, but does not record it). ''What grade are you in?'' (The tester listens to the response, but does not record it). ''Are you good at making things with your hands?'' (The tester listens to the response, and records to the right of the question either ''Y'' for a ''yes'' response or ''N'' for a ''no'' response. The tester then proceeds to the next question).

Scoring:

The responses are scored according to the key. Responses that do not correspond to the key are ''negative'' responses, indicating a low self-concept on a given response. These ''negative'' responses are totaled.

TABLE 27: *Self-opinion test*

QUESTIONS AND KEY

	Per cent		Per cent
1. Are you good at making things with your hands?	(33)*	Y	(27)†
2. Can you draw well?	(40)	Y	(27)
3. Are you strong?	(60)	Y	(33)
4. Do you like the way you look?	(13)	Y	(33)
5. Do your friends make fun of you?	(71)	N	(67)
6. Are you handsome/pretty?	(40)	Y	(27)
7. Do you have trouble making friends?	(47)	N	(43)
8. Do you like school?	(13)	Y	(13)
9. Do you wish you were different?	(33)	N	(27)
10. Are you sad most of the time?	(13)	N	(13)
11. Are you the last to be chosen in games?	(33)	N	(33)
12. Do girls like you?	(47)	Y	(40)
13. Are you a good leader in games and sports?	(20)	Y	(20)
14. Are you clumsy?	(33)	N	(33)
15. In games do you watch instead of play?	(27)	N	(20)
16. Do boys like you?	(47)	Y	(47)
17. Are you happy most of the time?	(13)	Y	(13)
18. Do you have nice hair?	(6)	Y	(13)
19. Do you play with younger children a lot?	(47)	N	(47)
20. Is reading easy for you?	(67)	Y	(47)

*Per cent of 15 children participating in a program for the remediation of motor problems giving *negative* responses to each question. Average age 8.0 years, (SD 2.23), 13 boys, 2 girls.

† Per cent of *negative* responses on the scale by the same group *after* a program of perceptual-motor education.

Adapted with permission of Ellen Piers.

TABLE 28: *Physical fitness tests*

ADMINISTRATION AND SCORING PROCEDURES

General consideration: The tester should describe each movement, and permit the child to respond. The child should arise after each request.

Testing:

a. Push-Ups: The tester should place himself on the mat in a front-lying position: feet together, legs rigid; hands shoulder width apart. He should bend his arms at the elbows, lowering his chest to the mat, and then push on the mat with his hands to finish the movement. He should repeat this movement twice, and say, "Now you try it as many times as you can in twenty seconds." The tester should note whether or not the child's back is straight in recording the number of push-ups.

b. Sit-Ups: The tester should position himself on the mat in a back-lying position, with the soles of his feet on the mat at hip width and with his legs bent at the knees. He should then lie back on the mat and clasp both hands behind his neck. He should attempt to sit up without moving his legs, and then lower his back again to the mat. He should repeat this movement twice, and say, "Now you try it as many times as you can in twenty seconds." When the child seats himself on the mat in a back-lying position, with the soles of his feet on the mat at hip width and with his legs bent at the knees, the tester should hold the child's ankles. The tester should record the number of sit-ups done by the child without moving his legs.

c. Pull-Ups: The tester tells the child to lie on his back on the mat. The tester stands over the child, facing the child, with his feet spread on both sides of the child. The tester grasps the bar with both hands held at the middle of the bar, held at the child's arms length. "Now I want you to grab both ends of the bar." When the child obeys, the tester says, "Now without moving your heels and keeping your body straight, I want you to pull yourself up to the bar using only your arms so that your chin touches the bar. Do it as many times as you can in twenty seconds." The number of pull-ups done by using only the arms, and not moving the heels and keeping the body straight, are recorded.

d. Reverse Sit-Ups: The tester should position himself on the mat on his stomach, with his arms stretched perpendicularly from his trunk and with his legs straight back. He should then raise his upper body off the mat by tightening his hips and his lower back, and by keeping his arms and legs rigid. The tester should say, "Now you try it for as long as you can in twenty seconds. The number of seconds in which the child is able to keep his upper body off the mat by tightening his hips and lower back, and by keeping his arms and legs rigid, should be recorded to a maximum of twenty seconds.

TABLE 29: *Comparison of pre- and post-fitness scores by 65 children taking part in a five-month program designed to remediate their moderate motor problems.* *

	Pre-Test		Post-Test		
	M	σ	M	σ	t
PUSH-UPS	7.24	4.11	9.33	3.32	4.19
SIT-UPS	4.78	3.59	6.37	3.51	4.04
PULL-UPS	3.11	3.29	5.80	3.90	4.86
REVERSE SIT-UPS	14.37	6.71	17.00	4.73	2.93

*Average age 8.9 years, SD 2.48, 57 boys and 8 girls.

Index